STEP UP
The Accidental Manager's Guide to Leading a Team

MARION PARRISH

i

Printed in the United Kingdom.

First printing 2021

ISBN - 978-1-7398634-0-1 (Paperback)

ISBN - 978-1-7398634-1-8 (eBook)

Marion Parrish, The Accidental Manager Coach

Nottingham, NG10 3BU

www.marionparrish.com

DEDICATION

Thank you to all the managers I have worked for in the past. You taught me so much. While you thought you were teaching me the technicalities of being a good HR manager, the most valuable thing I learned was how managers can make their employees think and feel, and how this affects the way those employees behave and perform. For better or for worse.

And especially to Nigel and Steve, who seemed to know implicitly how to do HR, and people management, so well. My heartfelt thanks for giving me such a great start to my career in HR.

To Jonathan, Bethany, and Eloise, who always believed I had a book in me, and so much more. Thank you for your unending support.

To Alison, Jill, Judy, Kev and Vicky, thank you for your valuable feedback, which has made this book so much better than it might have been.

And to those I love who won't get to read this book. Never forgotten x

This book is dedicated to you all.

CONTENTS

INTRODUCTION

A lot changes when you become a manager.

The most obvious change is the team you now manage. Maybe you were a member of that team before your promotion, and you consider those you worked with as friends. Friends you will now supervise.

Perhaps when you became a manager for the first time you inherited a team from another manager, and whether that manager was good, bad, or indifferent, they will have left their own influence on the team, which may or may not fit with your approach.

You could be a new manager in a start-up business, trying to create order in a rapidly changing organisation.

Or maybe you are a business owner, building your own team from scratch, and must decide on everything from the culture you want to create, to the people you will need to deliver that culture.

You may feel excited as well as a little nervous about managing a team. Or you may be terrified of saying the wrong thing or doing the wrong thing, which could get yourself and your organisation into all sorts of trouble.

Maybe your team members like you, and maybe they don't. No doubt the feelings are mutual, and at some point, you'll let each other know you think you could do each other's jobs better.

And perhaps you feel lonely. Because it's a tough job sometimes, and it's not like you can go and have a moan with your team about how useless the manager is, when you are that manager!

As much as you thought you were ready to be a manager, it's unlikely you were fully prepared for just how much has changed. Or how different you feel about going to work, and the colleagues you work with, now that you are a manager.

Feelings matter a lot in the workplace.

Managers who feel anxious – about whether they are saying or doing the right things, or whether they can trust their team to do what they should be doing – will find managing people difficult. They will always be second-guessing themselves. "Should I say this, or will I get into trouble?" "Is it alright if I do that, or will my team think I have an ulterior motive?" "Why do my team never do what I ask them to do? Should I sack them all and start again?"

Whereas confident managers have a quiet authority that others recognise and respect. Their boundaries are clear, meaning the team understand the behaviours and performance expected of them. These managers know what they know – and most importantly, they know when to ask for help. Furthermore, they have clear routines, and systems, so they know exactly what each member of their team can do, and what they are still learning to do.

When team members feel valued and respected, and they understand what is expected of them, they work harder. Study after study shows this to be true. When they feel unappreciated, or they lack direction or feel ignored, they stop working as well. In the worst cases they become disruptive, and start making life very difficult for those around them.

And the person who impacts most on the way the team feel about their work is you – their manager.

In this book I am going to show you how you can help to make those feelings positive – or negative.

Or to put it another way. How you can make your life as a manager easier, and your team more productive, through simple things like understanding your own role, having the right conversations at the right time, getting to know the person behind the job, giving clear direction, and being personally organised.

What is an Accidental Manager?

To become a manager, you must already be pretty good at some things. I imagine you are extremely good at building a business and finding new clients, and your business has grown to a point where you can't handle any more work on your own. Or maybe you were brilliant at your day job, and the only way to earn more was to take a promotion, which involved managing a team. Perhaps you were the only person in your organisation qualified to take on a management role, and so here you are as a manager, with no real idea of what to do or why.

If this is how you became responsible for a team, you are probably an accidental manager. You didn't plan to lead a team. It wasn't what you started your business for, or in your career plan, but it was a by-product of your success. Now you have a team and they are looking to you for direction, support, and answers.

You aren't just managing yourself anymore, and your focus isn't just the work your own manager gives to you.

You now have the responsibility for managing other people, for making sure they have enough work to do each day, and that they do get on and do that work to the standard required.

Some in your team might be wondering why you got the job rather than them. They might remember you as the apprentice who joined the company years after they did, and who has somehow beaten them to a senior position. They may know more than you do about many aspects of the team's work, and you may feel that they aren't going to respect you very much as a result.

And I don't suppose they taught you how to handle any of that at school, college, or university, or even in your previous role. Because, according to the Chartered Management Institute, around 70% of British managers have never had a day's training on how to manage people in their lives. And that is a shame, because managing people is something you can learn how to do fairly quickly. There are certain key tasks and activities which, performed regularly, will make your life easier.

Learning to manage people is a bit like playing a musical instrument. There are lots of different elements that you must practice individually before they can be put together, and you might feel quite awkward as you are learning each part. You might wonder how on earth it all fits together, or whether it will ever be worth all the effort. But when you finally feel confident enough to put it all together you can suddenly see how each part is critical to the end result, and how leaving one element out diminishes the whole effect.

Good managers practice all the time, and learn from their mistakes. They understand that it can take a lifetime to understand people and get the best from them. They also know that practice makes perfect, and perseverance will win the day.

Sometimes you'll do something right, your team will love you for it, and for a few seconds you might start to think managing people is easy. But most of the time you probably find it really challenging.

This book is here to help you understand that you are in control. Whatever it might feel like to be an accidental manager, and whatever you think about the power your team seem to exert, YOU are in control.

Not in an overbearing, or autocratic way. Control doesn't mean you have to be bossy, or rule over your team like some medieval tyrant. It is more about being the one who decides on the direction of the team, sets the boundaries, manages the team's productivity, and knows the right thing to say, at the right time, to get the results you want.

The secret to managing a team successfully is – on paper - quite straightforward. It is to be crystal-clear about yourself, your role, what matters (and what doesn't) and how to be the manager that every person in your team needs you to be.

- It means facing up to sometimes difficult truths about yourself, and those who work for you and with you.
- It requires you to change the way you think about yourself, your business, and your team. About what work is, how work should be done, and how the people who do the work should be treated.
- And you'll need to ask yourself difficult questions, and be prepared to deal with the answers in a constructive way.

Management isn't easy. But it isn't impossible either. And with a clear understanding of the control you have, and the mindset you need, plus the determination to make it work, you can do it.

And I'm here to help you.

I've worked with over a thousand managers in my career, helping each of them to understand how to manage people more effectively. Many were brand new managers, recently promoted or appointed to a management role for the first time. Some were business owners who realised that the way they managed their team was preventing their business from growing successfully. Others were more experienced, all the way up to executive director level in large organisations.

Whatever level you are at, you will be facing similar challenges.

- How to get the best from the people in your team – especially those who don't seem to want to work as hard as you'd like them to?
- How to cope with all the different demands on your time, while still having time for a personal life?
- How to be a good manager and treat people well, without becoming a pushover?
- How to row back when you have let things slide too far?
- How to manage difficult people who just don't want to cooperate?
- How to feel confident when dealing with team issues, even when you have never encountered a particular issue before?
- How to work effectively with your own manager, and show them you are capable in your role as a team manager?

Whatever industry you are in, and however different you think your industry is from others, the way you manage people does not change. People are people. They are all different, and they all seem to want different things from their work and their manager. Nevertheless, fundamentally they all want the same things. To feel valued for their contribution, to have a sense of purpose in their work, to be listened to by the people around them, and to be treated fairly compared to their colleagues.

It sounds simple, yet many managers find these four needs really challenging to deliver. I think it's because they see management as a series of HR processes designed to trip them up along the way. I believe the key to success as a manager is to get to know the people who report to you, and understand how they are similar, or different to you. If you can do that, everything else then falls into place.

How this book is structured.

This isn't your average HR or management text book. You won't find a section on managing absence, or what to do if someone in your team raises a grievance.

Because as I said above, I don't believe management is – or ever should be - just about processes. Managers who manage the way I recommend don't usually need to use many of the more difficult HR processes, because they rarely encounter challenging HR issues. So, I have structured this book to reflect the way I coach accidental managers who want to manage people more effectively.

We're going to start by looking at why we need managers, and how your management approach impacts the way your team performs. I'll bust some myths about management, and then look at some of the changes you can expect to happen – for yourself and for your team - when you become a truly effective manager.

Understanding the context of your own role in your organisation is critical too, because the type of organisation you work for will heavily influence the kind of manager you can be, or need to be. We'll look at your own skills and attributes, the organisation you work in, and the team you manage.

All the way through, I'll be giving you tips and ideas of different things you could do to help you feel more confident and effective as a manager.

Finally, we will look at four big topics for new managers. How to structure your time effectively, so you can fit in all the important conversations and other routines you need to complete regularly. The challenges of managing remote teams, and working with other managers, both your own and managers at the same level as you. We'll consider how to recruit the right people, and answer some questions about employment law.

So, by the end of this book, you will have a whole new way of thinking about management, and the tools to help you Step Up into your new role.

CHAPTER 1
HOW YOU MANAGE MATTERS

Accidental managers usually fall into a management position without a plan. And without a plan, and some clear ideas of what kind of manager you want to be, it is easy to become overwhelmed by all the "stuff" that falls into a manager's inbox. Sometimes to the point where you have so many things to do, and so many ideas about how to improve things within your team, that you just don't know where to start.

What do you do when everything is top priority, urgent, and needed to be done yesterday? When there just aren't enough hours in the day to fit it all in, and all you can do is become increasingly worried and agitated that you just aren't doing this job the way you really want to be doing it?

As a manager, you aren't being paid to be busy all the time. You are being paid to manage. And the best managers do one thing very, very well.

They reflect. On their own performance. On how their team have performed. On what went better than expected, and what didn't go to plan. On how long things took, and what the manager and team learned from the experience. Great managers do this kind of reflection on most days. It helps them understand what works and what doesn't for the individuals in their team.

I am going to help you reflect, throughout this book, about the way you and your team work together. And the first thing we are going to reflect on, is how you want the people in your team to feel about working for you.

Let's start by looking at two opposing ways of managing people. As you read these descriptions, which one is closest to your own view of management? Which approach do you think would work best for your team?

Two ways of managing – and two different results

In my experience managers sit somewhere between two extremes.

On the one hand we have the manager who wants to get the job done, and has precious little time for anyone or anything that gets in the way. This type of manager thinks the key to business success is to hire people cheaply (often on minimum wage) and extract every last ounce of value from them, before the employee becomes completely disillusioned and leaves for another job which might pay an extra 20p an hour. This manager thinks that being a good leader means making sure employees understand their place, which is to do exactly what the manager requests, without question.

There is very little flexibility from managers at this extreme, and any that exists is wholly in the manager's favour. Stuck in traffic because of an accident on the way to work? Better catch up at lunchtime. Want time off to watch a school play? Too bad, we're too busy. But of course, the employee is expected to stay behind at the end of the day if there is a deadline to hit. Unpaid, naturally.

Unsurprisingly, in environments like this there are usually high levels of absence. People usually don't want to come to work, and the stress and toxicity of the environment lead to increased incidences of genuine illness, as well as ad hoc absences from those who just can't face another day in such a difficult workplace.

These managers spend their time using HR processes to maintain control of their teams. They need to show their workforce who is boss by making sure that anyone who takes more than the prescribed number of days off sick, or anyone who is late more than the accepted number of times, is dealt with strictly according to "the process".

I find it interesting that everyone who follows this "people are dispensable" approach thinks they are being fair and they are getting the best value from their employees. Most would say they are good managers.

The truth is they are wrong. In every way.

The costs of managing like this are obvious when you think about it, although most managers who follow this way of managing never appear to see them.

You will never have a choice of good applicants to work in your business, because the pay is so poor. So, the calibre of your employees will match the pay you offer. Those employees will know they are poorly paid, so will downgrade their performance to match what you are paying. They will work to the letter of their contracts so they don't lose their jobs, but they won't do any more than they have to, because they aren't rewarded for it. They'll watch others come and go, and understand that the organisation doesn't care who is doing the job, as long as the job gets done. And when an employee has to undergo a course of medical treatment, and finds the absence management process is subsequently used against them, they will understand that the employer doesn't care about them either. They'll warn their friends off applying for jobs with you, because it's such a toxic place to work, limiting even further the pool of candidates for your vacancies.

And when the chips are down, when things are going really badly at work and the manager needs everyone to help out, these employees will stand back, look at their manager, and shrug their shoulders.

And who could blame them?

At the other extreme of the management continuum are those who make management look like hard work – and expensive work at that. They value people above process. That doesn't mean the job isn't important – far from it. But these managers put most of their effort into the people, believing that if you get the people side right, everything else follows.

That means they offer competitive, or even above average salary rates. Or if the business really can't afford to pay well, they provide lower-than-average pay alongside something else that employees will value - like supportive management, a great culture, training, experience, career progression, flexible working, social activities, or other perks.

As a result, they attract candidates who value these things. Who want to work with like-minded individuals and learn from their manager and colleagues. Who value developing their skills, and soak up opportunities to try new activities and learn new ways of working. Who want to be treated as adults, with individual needs and personal lives, and have a joint stake in the success of the business.

The manager's top priority is to get to know each person in the team – what drives them, what grounds them, what they really want from work, what their strengths are, and what they need from the organisation in order to stay. And the manager will see to it that those things are delivered.

Attracting new recruits is easy in this environment. Employees tell their friends and relatives what a great place they work in, and those friends and relatives are queuing up to apply. Along with other equally ambitious, highly skilled candidates who want to work somewhere they can continue to develop their skills.

And when employees understand this is the culture they are working in, that their contribution is valued, and that they have a stake in the success or failure of the company, their attitude mirrors the manager's priorities. When things get difficult for the business, they roll up their sleeves and suggest ways of helping the company out of the mess they are in.

I'll be honest. I'm a big fan of finding the easiest and most cost-effective way to do any task or achieve any result. So, I make no apologies whatsoever for being an ardent promoter of the second way of managing. It just makes sound business sense.

It costs less, because when people join they will stay, so you aren't in a permanent recruitment cycle.

It's easier, because team members want to do all they can to help the business succeed.

Employees don't need constant supervision, because they are motivated to give their best at everything they do.

It takes less management time because there are very rarely any HR problems to manage. The time investment from the manager is in the conversations, the getting to know people, and the coaching of team members to help them achieve their full potential. They find the time to do this because they aren't tied up managing conflict or disciplinary situations.

Management in an organisation like this is about finding opportunities to help people grow. Identifying talent and making sure it is used for the benefit of the organisation, which in turn will also benefit the employee. It's more about coaching and supporting people, and enabling them to be the best that they can be.

And most importantly, as a manager you are growing all the time because you are constantly learning about better ways to manage people and develop your team.

Can the way I manage really make that much difference?

When I say the way you manage matters, I'm speaking from the heart. I've been there, with some of the best managers I could ever imagine having the privilege to work for. People who supported me and stretched me and challenged me to be more than I ever dreamed it was possible to be. Accidental managers who were willing to admit what they didn't know, and who were open to learning new approaches and new ways of doing things. Managers who trusted me to do tasks way beyond my paygrade, because they believed in my ability far more than I did. Managers who pushed me to take the next step in my career because they believed I was ready, long before I believed it myself. Managers who made coming to work feel like fun. We would have a laugh, even on the worst days, because they didn't take themselves too seriously.

I worked damned hard for those managers. And I was happy to do it. I stayed late, took work home and did it in my own time, came in early, volunteered to do more, took on tasks outside my responsibility, and researched around topics in my own time so I could be more effective during my working hours. Modesty prevents me from making the judgement myself, but I'd say in many respects I was what most employers would describe as the perfect employee.

And I've had my share of managers who were horrors. The worst were the accidental managers who had worked their way up the organisation with a great big chip on their shoulders. Maybe that chip was the qualifications they didn't have, or their belief that they owed their success to family connections rather than merit, or the realisation that their team had more experience than they did.

Whatever the reason, they could never admit they didn't know how to manage people effectively. Those managers spent their working days afraid of others discovering their weaknesses.

I've had managers who:

- Were scared to let go of work so they didn't share timely information that would help the team work more effectively.
- Micromanaged others because they couldn't bear to lose control.
- Judged everyone by the time they spent at their desks, rather than the work they produced.
- Were always right, even when proved wrong, or who would tell barefaced, blatant lies to their team and their own manager, to cover their own inadequacies.
- Thought shouting at people in the middle of the office was preferable to a quiet word in a private room.
- Only felt good when they had someone in the team in tears, or too scared to speak.
- Were so disengaged and disillusioned with working life they abdicated all responsibility for their team.
- Spent more time playing organisational politics than leading meaningful change.

And guess what? The work I did for those managers was the minimum it took to stay out of trouble. If they wanted to clock-watch, so would I. If they wanted to correct every piece of work I did, I wouldn't bother to make sure it was perfect because I knew they would pick up any errors. No interest in team activities or projects because what was the point? The manager would just take over and do it their way anyway. And I wouldn't work a single minute more than I had to. I kept my head down, did what I had to do, and didn't care about doing anything extra.

Same person, but a completely different worker depending on the manager I worked for. Maybe closer to your idea of a nightmare employee? The person who was obviously coasting, disinterested, unmotivated and wasting their skills and talents.

And the biggest problem for me when working for terrible managers was the impact it had on my own self-confidence and self-esteem. When someone is constantly criticising what you do, you start to believe that you can't do even simple things properly. When your manager doesn't give you information until the last minute and you don't have time to act on it, it chips away at your confidence and you become even more certain that you have lost your basic skills. And when someone tells you something is true that you absolutely know is not, well, at some point you start to question your own sanity and memory. You think it is evidence of something else you can't do anymore.

It happened to me. And it is happening across the British workforce, in workplace after workplace. Toxic managers are destroying the confidence of the people who work for them, and in return our productivity is lower than just about any other major economy. Large sectors of our workforce are disinterested while many employees are facing burnout because of the high demands placed on them during the Covid-19 pandemic and the subsequent economic recovery.

Some companies experience such high levels of staff turnover and blame it all on British workers not wanting to work. I say that isn't true. People just don't want to work for nightmare managers who undervalue them and make their working lives a living hell.

And HR professionals are not helping. My profession loves its rigid procedures and policies that stifle the life and spirit out of everyone and ensure that no-one can give their best to their job. HR – as practised by some – has become so risk averse that the answer in most cases is "no". HR solutions to problems are so complicated, so convoluted, that most line managers just don't bother trying. You might as well put up with a poor performer when you look at the effort it is going to take to change that situation.

So, as you think about the culture of your business, and your team, instead of a race to the bottom, what about a race to the top? What if, instead of focusing on how cheaply we can produce things, we start focusing on how well we serve customers? What if we forget about trying to undercut suppliers, or keep down the pay bill, and instead think about how to deliver great quality with motivated, highly skilled staff?

What if we really worked towards creating workplaces that your ideal employees never want to leave?

If you want to be a good manager, focus on the people. When people feel valued at work, and truly appreciated as the unique individuals they are, they will deliver the job for you every time. They will see it as a matter of pride and honour to do so. They will feel they owe it to you, because you have been so good and so fair to them.

Who wouldn't want to manage people like this?

And you can. With the right mindset, and the right knowledge about yourself, your team, and your business, with a little sprinkling of good HR practice, you could be that kind of manager.

CHAPTER 2
MYTHS ABOUT MANAGEMENT

Everyone has an opinion about management. Which means you hear a lot of truth, and a lot of fiction about life as a manager. Here are some of my favourite myths, and the reason why I think each one is wrong.

Anyone can do it – it's a natural progression up the career ladder

This is the biggest myth of all. And unfortunately, it's the most widely believed myth, which explains why so few accidental managers have had any training about managing people.

Most people are promoted to management positions because they are the best person at doing their day job. They quickly find that there is nothing natural about the move from being a technical specialist to being a manager of people.

Look at it this way. If you grew up wanting to be a scientist, or an IT specialist, or an engineer, you probably spent years of your life learning about your speciality. You went on courses, watched TV programmes and films, read books and had long, in depth conversations about your passion with anyone who would listen. If it takes 10,000 hours to become an expert in something, many of us probably put those hours into our chosen career without even realising it through magazine or journal articles we read, the websites we visited, the experiments we did, or the experts we spoke or listened to.

And in your 10,000+ hours, you will have learnt skills such as researching, perseverance, self-motivation, analysing data, self-management, time management, resilience, how to learn, teamwork, creativity, using technology, communication, flexibility, project management…the list goes on and on.

And all those skills will be very useful to you as a manager. But when you lead a team, you also need other skills. Leadership, conflict management, empathy, negotiation, planning, delegation, motivating others, and communicating to people at different levels.

And the chances are that, with all that time invested in learning your specialist area, there wasn't much time left for learning how to manage people. Why would there be? If your passion is science, that's what you will focus on – not management.

However, when you get to the point where you can't grow your business any further without employing extra help, or you can't get any more money from your employer without taking a promotion into team management, suddenly you find yourself being an expert in your chosen field, and an absolute novice at managing people. And because you are so experienced at your technical role, you've probably forgotten what it felt like to know very little about something. How awkward it feels to be faced with challenges that you have no idea how to resolve. And how stressful that feeling of not knowing can be.

The very best managers know they still have a lot to learn, and seek help to learn this information as quickly and effectively as they can. It may be by reading books like this, or going on training courses, or being coached or mentored by a more experienced manager or an HR professional like me.

The key to learning quickly on the job is to make sure you build in a lot of time for reflection. Time that you can spend pondering why some problems seem to occur repeatedly, and how your actions might be contributing to those problems. You can reflect by yourself, but working with someone else will enable you to think more deeply about the issues or situations you encounter, and find the lessons in them that will help you continuously improve your management abilities.

You can't be kind, and be an effective manager

If you are a manager you need to be prepared for some tough decisions. They come with the job unfortunately. Decisions about who will work where, and what they will do. Who will be promoted, and who won't? Where to cut costs? Who to make redundant? When to close the business?

Every decision involving people is a difficult decision. There is nothing I can say or tell you that will change the fact that your decisions will often change people's lives. The choices you make at work might be the difference between whether someone loves their job or hates it, sees their children before bedtime or doesn't, feels happy and fulfilled or stressed and miserable. Your decisions might be blamed (by your team) for their financial difficulties, marital problems, children's behavioural problems, mental health problems, physical health problems, not seeing their baby born or their parent in hospital. Basically, for the end of their world as they know it.

And there may be an element of truth in their view.

You can't back away from the difficult decisions. You're being paid to make them, after all. But you can be a human about the way you implement decisions.

- You don't have to announce redundancies the week before Christmas – or the week after.
- You don't have to enforce a job change on someone who doesn't want to move.
- No-one is forcing you to dismiss a pregnant worker.
- You don't need to see a death certificate to let someone have bereavement leave.
- You don't need to overload people with work until they become too ill to do any of it.

It is very rare in business – as in life - that decisions must be made at a specific point in time with no forewarning. And each decision you make is a choice. You can choose how, and when, you make the decision, and you can choose whether you make that decision easy for you to deliver, or easy for the other person to accept. There is a difference.

Consideration doesn't cost anything. Thinking about how someone feels, and delivering your decisions in a caring, thoughtful, and respectful way is not being weak. On the contrary, it is showing basic empathy and gratitude for someone who has probably given you several years' service, made you a lot of money over that time, and frankly deserves better than being pulled into the office on a Friday afternoon to be "let go".

And think very hard about the way you treat employees who become pregnant, or disabled, or just go through a really difficult time in their personal lives, perhaps because of financial difficulties, marital problems, ill health, or family bereavement. Because these are difficult situations for you as a business owner or team manager too. Your previously reliable, flexible employee might start taking time off work unexpectedly, or be unable to travel for a while. Perhaps their decision-making becomes a bit unpredictable, they seem distracted when they are at work, or a previously good-natured employee starts snapping at colleagues and customers.

Treating people with care and respect, as humans, is the hallmark of a great manager. If an employee has given you good service during their years of employment with you then, frankly, you owe them some support as they go through difficult times in their personal lives.

I hear so many employees in roles that are not well paid and don't carry many prospects, express such loyalty towards their employer because of the way the employer stood by them during pregnancy, maternity, ill health, parental illness and all the family dramas that we all encounter over our lives. It really is worth putting people's feelings first when making difficult decisions.

Make the decision, but do it with care, empathy, and consideration, not cruelty and speed.

If a team member doesn't agree completely with you, it's their problem

Do you remember when you were at school, struggling over a problem in a maths lesson? Your teacher would have explained on the board how to perform the calculation, and you would think you understood what they were talking about. Then when you came to do the work yourself you would find those pesky numbers just didn't seem to work out the way the teacher had made them work. The answer you got just didn't make any sense.

As you look back on that situation now, who do you think was responsible for making sure you understood how to do your maths problem?

There's no question it was the teacher's job to communicate the method in a way that everyone in the class could understand. And if, after the first explanation, half the class couldn't do the equation, it was the teacher's responsibility to find a different way of explaining the technique, a way that those pupils who hadn't originally got it could comprehend.

And if there were still a few strugglers, it was the teacher's job to find another way to explain the method she wanted the class to use. And another way, and another way, until everyone understood.

As a manager, you have the responsibility for making sure your team understand what they should be doing, where the organisation is going, and how they should behave and perform while they are at work. If someone in your team thinks you have got things wrong, your role is to listen and understand their concerns, and either change your mind (if they give you a reason to do so) or explain to them again why you believe your way is correct. And you may need to find more than one way of explaining yourself, just like that maths teacher, because all your employees are different, their minds work differently, they process information differently, and you need to work out the best way of communicating to each of them so that they understand.

What is logical to you, based on the information you have and your understanding of the workplace, might make no sense whatsoever to your team who don't have the same information or experience. You may have made a decision that makes their working life more difficult (we've all had that happen) or which changes a fundamental part of their role that matters a lot to them.

My experience is that 99.9% of problem employees are problems because of something their manager has said or done, or not said or not done.

- That employee who was promised at their interview they would be promoted within a year of joining, but was later told that a reorganisation would take the job away.
- The team member who has asked you to help them resolve a particular work problem that is causing them stress, or making their job more difficult, that you never have the time to support.

- The person you promised a training course, or a new computer to speed up their work, and then you didn't get around to organising it, or
- You agreed to "flexible working", yet made sure it was only ever flexible in favour of the employer, not the employee.

All these seemingly small oversights or changes create disappointment, resentment, and the overwhelming feeling that the manager doesn't have their backs.

When these things happen, and employees stop agreeing with their managers or stop cooperating with new tasks, both parties take some responsibility.

But most of it sits with the manager who didn't communicate clearly, or didn't deliver what they promised.

Be clear, as a manager you have access to much more information than most of your team. If you own your business, then you know what your strategy is, what your values are and what acceptable employee behaviour looks like – even if you haven't articulated it yet. Whatever your situation, when an employee disagrees with you, it is usually a signal that you have either:

- Not explained yourself fully
- Assumed they knew some key piece of information that they don't know
- Made a decision without knowing something they do already know, or
- Contradicted a previous decision or instruction you have given.

Employees have the law on their side at work

There are a lot of laws that managers and business owners must follow when employing people, and those laws are there for one reason, and one reason only.

The only way to get some employers to give some very basic rights, is to pass laws to force the employers to do so.

Some of these "terrible" laws are:

- Producing a payslip to show what you have paid employees for the time they have worked, and the deductions you have made (or not) for tax, national insurance, or other reasons.
- Allowing people to take paid holiday from work.
- Preventing people from working more than 48 hours per week without their consent.
- Requiring employers to pay a minimum hourly rate to their employees.
- Requiring employers who want to dismiss an employee with more than 2 years' service to have a fair reason for dismissal and to follow a fair process.
- Encouraging people with disabilities to play an active role in society through working.

Would you really want to work in a business where these laws don't exist and employers can exploit workers, pay wages that don't support a family, have workers who are too tired to work safely or make good decisions, or who are terrified to step out of line in case they are dismissed?

The real reason why some employers think the law favours their employees, is that they don't communicate with each of their employees about expected standards of behaviour and performance, or keep adequate records of the conversations they have with their employees. Then when there is a problem, the employer "knows" there is an issue but can't prove it because they haven't bothered to keep any evidence. And therefore, they must start collecting the evidence at a point when they really should have taken disciplinary action.

The law is almost entirely on the employer's side. If you just follow a few basic principles, you can discipline or dismiss employees if you need to do so.

Those few basic principles?

- Have clear roles and responsibilities for each team member.
- Train your employees in the tasks you want them to do.
- Measure and monitor their performance and conduct regularly, and keep records.
- Tell them – regularly - how they are doing, how they compare to your expectations, and what to do differently.
- Provide coaching and support to help employees perform better.
- Keep records of your conversations, and if performance or conduct doesn't improve, start formal disciplinary procedures.

In reality, if you follow those few basic principles, you are very unlikely to need to discipline or dismiss employees, because you will be correcting their behaviour or performance as you go, and they will understand what you want and do their best to achieve it.

So, it really boils down to whether you'd prefer the pain of holding regular performance discussions with your team for an hour each month, or the agony of formal disciplinary hearings, dismissals and employment tribunals which will take at least a year of your life each time.

I know which I would recommend.

Managers command respect from their teams

I think this is something that most accidental managers find really difficult to get their heads around. Maybe you have experienced this – maybe it's why you picked up this book.

Let's just dispel this myth straight away.

Gone are the days when managers could insist on respect just because they were managers. You earn respect, it doesn't come automatically. It comes when you admit that you don't know everything, and ask the experts in the team for their advice. When you check your facts before making accusations. When you roll up your sleeves and help if the team have a difficult deadline to achieve.

When you are seen to consistently deliver what you have promised to do for your team members. When you have their backs, and don't let others blame them for your decisions. When they have learnt they can rely on you to react in the same way every time they raise an issue or bring you a problem. When they know they can trust you to do what you say, when you say it, and with their best interests at heart.

And you lose it when you say negative things about them behind their backs. When one day you accept mistakes as learning opportunities, and the next day a minor indiscretion causes you to lose your temper and berate your employee in front of their colleagues. When you make a fool of yourself or them by blagging about something you do not fully understand. When you make decisions without getting all the facts or listening to their advice. When you take the credit for their work, demand they work unreasonable hours because you are too disorganised to get things done on time, or give them tasks without all the information they need to get the job done.

Respect and trust are closely linked. When you lose one, you usually lose the other too. Or to quote an old Dutch proverb *"Trust arrives on foot, but leaves on horseback"*.

Managers need to work long hours to get the job done

There will, without doubt, be times that you have to work long hours. Workload in every organisation has its peaks and troughs, and there will always be times when you are busier than you might like to be. Perhaps your workload spikes at month-end and year-end, maybe you have projects to deliver to a deadline that doesn't move when things go wrong, or perhaps you are short-staffed. These are all natural times when you might expect to work longer hours than you would wish.

However, long hours shouldn't be a regular or permanent part of your role. They do not come with the territory of being a manager and you are not expected to deliver everything yourself. You have a team to help you with that, and part of your role is to work out how to best use each person in the team to help deliver the team's goals.

So if you are working long hours, you should ask yourself a few questions.

- Am I really organising my time as effectively as I could? Where is my time being spent?
- Am I certain what my priorities are? And what is not as important?
- Am I making the best use of the people in my team to help deliver the team's workload?
- Am I delegating work appropriately to the rest of my team?
- Am I working longer hours because I am compensating for someone else who isn't pulling their weight?
- Have I requested additional resources to help the team manage its workload within normal working hours?
- Am I saying yes to my own manager, or to my team, or to our clients, when I should be saying no?
- Am I choosing to work long hours because I don't want to go home?

Working long hours can quickly become a habit. And like most habits, once established it can be very difficult to break. So be very honest with yourself. If you are working longer hours because you think that's what managers do, ask yourself why you think you should work so many unpaid hours. You may find that the only person who truly believes you should work so long is you.

And if you are thinking that working long hours is showing your manager how committed you are to your role, you may be disappointed to discover the ultimate irony. The managers above you probably see your long hours as evidence that you aren't coping because you cannot do your job within your normal working hours.

We'll look at managing your time in more detail in the next chapter. For now, just think about the story you tell yourself about being a manager and working time, and be prepared to challenge that story.

CHAPTER 3
WHAT CHANGES WHEN YOU BECOME A MANAGER?

You don't wake up on the morning of your first day as a manager with a whole new range of skills and knowledge. There is no magic wand that transforms you into a completely different person. So why does it all feel so different when you become a manager? Where does your confidence disappear to? Why does it suddenly feel as though you are completely incompetent and unable to make the simplest of decisions?

What really changes is the way you think about yourself, your team, and your role as a manager. And they aren't always good and helpful thoughts. They can completely overwhelm you if you don't understand that they are perfectly normal, and that every other manager has had these thoughts or something very similar. Here are some of the ideas that might be weighing heavily on your mind when you become a manager.

Everyone is relying on you

Organisations need managers to make sure employees are doing the work they are employed to do. Managers are responsible for planning how and when to do the work, organising who will do it, and making sure their employees have everything they need to get the job done. They must control people, resources, and budgets so that work is done at a price the organisation can afford. Managers give instructions, and check the work has been done on time, then face the music from their own boss if things haven't gone to plan.

For employees, the most important workplace relationship is with their manager. No-one else has a greater impact on an employee's happiness, motivation, productivity, and self-confidence than the person who directly line manages them.

There's an old saying that people join companies and leave managers. And survey after survey suggests that saying is true. An applicant in a busy jobs market has little option but to make their decision about where they might like to work based on the website, products and services or glossy brochures of the recruiting company. Once they start working, the reality of life inside the organisation hits home. The person they have most contact with during their working time is their manager. The manager who is the gatekeeper for information, reward, recognition, and progression. Get on well with the manager, and working life is just peachy. Find a manager whose core values and beliefs turn out to be very different to the applicant's own, and it's a very different scenario.

It's a tough gig, being a manager. You must recruit, train, motivate, coach, monitor, correct, support, develop, discipline, and keep occupied a team of different personalities with different strengths and different attitudes. You also have to keep your own boss happy, and regularly report to your own manager the progress you and your team are making. You need to be a problem-solver, a fire-fighter, a listening ear, a bum-kicker, and a counsellor, often all in the same afternoon.

People are relying on you – that much is true. And however much pressure you put on yourself to be the fount of all knowledge, your team don't expect you to know everything immediately, or to solve all the problems your team face overnight. Take things at a sensible pace, and don't let the thought of all these expectations overwhelm you. You can only do your best, and it takes time to be a confident manager.

You discover you can't manage everyone the same way

If you want an easier life as a manager, then just focus on being the right boss for the workers who report to you. And the way to be the right boss is to work out who you have working in your team, and what they need from you as their manager.

It means, to an extent, that you must get inside your team members' heads. Understand what drives them, what worries them, what frustrates them. Make it your business to know what else is going on in their lives. You don't have to do this in an overbearing, nosey kind of way. Just be interested in what they tell you. Ask them what they did at the weekends. Be alert to changes in their behaviour or appearance that might indicate something is going on at home. Think, all the time, about how they might be interpreting your requests, and adjust your approach to make sure their interpretation will match your intentions.

And if you're wondering, then yes – that means you need to be a different manager for each person who works for you. Some will need lots of support and reassurance. Some will need a firm approach, with clearly defined boundaries and sanctions if things go wrong. Some will need you to be directive – to tell them what to do and then when they have done it to tell them what to do next. Some will just want you to give them something to do and leave them to get on with it. You might have to be all these things in the space of an afternoon. And even more confusingly, the same person might need a free hand for some types of work, and their hand holding for another task.

So, put aside for a while any misconceptions you have about having to treat everyone the same… to be a great boss, you will be treating each person in your team in the way they need to be treated to enable them to give their best at work. And it is quite possible to do this within the law, in case you were wondering! We'll talk more about this later.

You find out who your friends are

Your mates were probably delighted for you when they heard about your promotion. And you probably thought it would be a nice first step into management, taking charge of the team you used to work in.

Big mistake!

Stepping up to manage the team you were once part of is the hardest promotion you will ever experience.

Anyone who has tried it will tell you it is a huge challenge.

You go from being everyone's mate, sitting in the break area moaning about your manager, to being the manager your so-called friends all moan about.

Where you used to be able to confide in people and tell them about your problems at home or at work, suddenly it doesn't seem appropriate any more, and even if it did, they don't want to hear about it now. They become suspicious about why you are telling them this stuff, whether you are looking for some sympathy, and why you think they are going to sympathise with you now you're all la-di-dah and earning a nice fat salary. Or worse, they remember what you have said and use it later to try and undermine you or make you feel more vulnerable.

They still go out together in a group for nights out, but you realise that if you go with them it won't be quite the same as before. What if they start behaving inappropriately – as their manager, you might have to take some formal action back in the workplace.

What if you get drunk? Can you trust yourself not to say anything you shouldn't? Not to divulge any confidential information you are now privy to?

Your best friends might expect you to do them some favours – turn a blind eye if they are late, let them off if they don't achieve their performance targets, overlook their absences, go easy on them. And if you do follow company policies and take them to task, they probably won't take you seriously.

I've known several managers who have stayed very close to their best friends after the manager's promotion, and then have found themselves with a real moral dilemma. In one case the employee had confided in the manager (outside of work) that she hadn't really been ill when she called in sick for work on several occasions over the previous month. She had been taking time off to help her partner with his new business.

Now, as a manager, and a best friend, once you know something like that, what on earth do you do?

The best friend would keep their mouth shut and support their friend. Obviously.

Except claiming company sick pay for days when you weren't genuinely ill is a serious offence in most companies. If you're caught defrauding the Company sick pay scheme you can expect at least a formal disciplinary warning, and are very likely to be dismissed for gross misconduct.

So now you, the manager, know that your best friend has committed this offence and broken a company rule. And you know the penalty for breaking that rule can be dismissal. You only know about the offence because they confided in you, their best friend.

Though, as a manager, you also have a responsibility to your employer to deal with breaches of company rules using formal disciplinary procedures.

So, are you going to drop your best friend in it? Or risk your own career by keeping it quiet?

There is no easy answer. And some managers will argue there isn't a right answer either. Because there is one answer if you are a friend, and a different answer if you are a manager.

If you are both, then what you have is a huge headache. To fulfil your employment contract/job description you must disclose what you know to your own manager. To be a friend you must keep quiet.

And it isn't an isolated case. I know managers who have had to make their best friend redundant, and managers who have been the subject of grievances because they didn't make their best friends redundant when others in the team lost their jobs. Many managers have had to discipline their best friend for breaching company rules. Imagine having to give your best friend a warning for absence while knowing that the absences were related to morning sickness due to undisclosed pregnancy. I've known managers who have had to mediate in disputes between their best friend and another team member (and realise that their best friend was in the wrong) and one poor team leader who had to tell his best friend's wife that an accident at work had killed her husband.

The emotional toll on these managers was tough, and all of them told me they wished they hadn't managed their best friends. And that is the main reason that I always recommend that managers are friendly with their teams, but not best friends. Putting a bit of distance between you and your team will enable you to be a manager when you need to be. It may also save you from accusations of favouritism, or finding your loyalties torn between your employer and your friendships.

If you are promoted into your first management job in the same company that you worked as a team member, you'll also find out very quickly that your whole support network at work basically disappears. All the people you used to be able to rely on and trust, suddenly don't trust you anymore. You might not even trust yourself to say or do the right things. The only person you can confide in is your manager – and you might not always want your manager to know how unsure or vulnerable you feel.

In short, it's no wonder new managers can feel very, very isolated. Promotion puts you up above the rest of the team – you become the target for their frustration with the company as well as the things you have said and done as their manager. They will say things to you, and about you, that they would never dream of saying to other team members at their own level.

Everything will be your fault.

So, the very first dilemma you face as a new manager, is deciding how you are going to handle this.

You could carry on as before. Continue to be friends with everyone, joining in with the team gossip, complaining about the company, going out at weekends, and sharing secrets with your friends/team. Of course, sharing secrets is a two-way thing, so you will have to share your own personal life with them, your hopes and fears, your frustrations with the company and your own manager, and everything else that goes with being part of the crowd.

And the flip-side of that is when you find yourself at opposite ends of the table in a discussion about someone's conduct at work, or their attendance or performance, how likely do you think it is that they will take you seriously? Could your best friend divulge those confidences you shared as part of their defence? It's a dangerous game and one that very few managers will win.

Another option is to remove yourself completely from all non-work interaction. You might see this as the nuclear approach. Instead of continuing your existing friendships, you drop everyone. Like a stone. You explain nicely that your new position makes it impossible for you to continue being friends, and you break all contact other than legitimate work-related interactions.

The advantage of this approach is clear – you are no longer at risk of compromising your position, you have put a clear boundary between you as the manager and the team you lead, and everyone knows who is in charge.

But you also set yourself up for a lonely life inside and outside work. Those water-cooler moments become stilted and polite, rather than an opportunity to build real relationships in the workplace. Your distance may become a problem if team members really need to confide something to you. They may hide problems that you could nip in the bud until they blow up into a crisis.

In short, not having any personal interaction has as many disadvantages as being too close. Neither option is ideal.

My preferred approach is to be friendly and go out together – while having your own personal limits.

The most effective teams can share a laugh and a joke together. They know enough about each other to be able to sympathise about family issues, challenge work-related decisions and lend a supportive ear when necessary, while also recognising who is in charge and when to fall in line with the manager. Social events can be a great way of breaking down barriers between team members, helping the team to communicate more effectively. So don't stop all social contact, but do think carefully about how you are going to approach the situation, and what your personal boundaries are.

My preference is to take part in team nights out or other social events

– up to a point. Two or three drinks, and then either move onto soft drinks and stay for the rest of the evening, or make your excuses and leave the rest of the team to have a good time together. Participate, show your human side, relax with the team a bit, but don't let alcohol affect your own judgement, and if you are concerned about the night getting out of hand, make sure you leave before the alcohol really starts affecting people's behaviour. After all, who is going to have to deal with the fallout from a drunken night out?

And yes, that means going out and getting very, very drunk with the team is one of those experiences you must confine to history. There is no point being nostalgic about it, or thinking you can be the manager who breaks the mould, the one who can balance being "one of the team" without calling your professionalism into question. You can't. It never ends well. It's best not to even try.

The middle ground is where you need to sit as a manager, being friendly but not expecting the sort of close friendships you may have had before. It is the price you pay for the position, the responsibility, and the reward of being a manager.

Your team will judge you, all the time

You have hundreds of "moments of truth" every day. Moments where something happens, you react, and your team make a judgement about you. Whether you were pleased or angry. Whether you know what you're doing or are out of your depth. Whether they believe you or think you are lying to them. Whether you were sympathetic or uncaring. Whether you have a sense of humour or are the most miserable person to walk the planet. Whether they can trust you or daren't tell you anything. And much more. And most of the time, you have no idea they are making those judgements, because you are just being you. But all the time, your team are jumping to conclusions about what that eye-roll or glance away or shoulder-shrug might mean.

You can't get it right all the time, and no-one expects you to. Still, if you get it wrong too often you will find yourself in an impossible position where no-one respects you anymore.

And getting yourself back from that position is a massive job.

For accidental managers, understanding that you are "on stage" all the time, with your team watching and judging everything you say and do, is the first step to learning how to manage your behaviour and your reactions, so that those judgements are a lot closer to the truth than they might otherwise be.

You manage your team's time as well as your own.

We looked at the myth that you have to work long hours as a manager in the previous chapter. But even if you don't work particularly long hours, it's likely you will find that life as a manager is busy. You will normally have a "day job" to do, as well as a team to manage.

You may be part of a management team, and you may have your own manager who has their own expectations about what you are employed to do, and what is an acceptable level of performance for you. Your company may ask you to take on special projects that sit outside your normal sphere of expertise, or to lead on particular areas on behalf of the management team.

So, unless you want to spend your evenings and weekends peering over your laptop at your family, pretending to be interested in what they are saying while you desperately try to finish the report for the next day's management meeting, you are going to have to find new ways to manage your time effectively.

So go back to your job description again.

What does your company pay you to do? What are the responsibilities listed in your job description that you absolutely must do?

Write them down.

Now look at your targets (assuming your manager has agreed some with you). Your organisation might call these goals, or objectives, or Key Performance Indicators (KPIs). You must deliver these if you wish to keep your job. So, write these down too. (If you have never heard of KPIs, I describe them in more detail in Chapter 5.)

And then there is your team. They are going to help you deliver your responsibilities and objectives/KPIs, and it is your job to manage them so that they can do so.

What do they need from you? At a very basic level, they are likely to need you to do the following:

- Allocate work so that they have enough to fill their working hours, and the business can deliver to customer deadlines.
- Monitor workloads, so that no-one has too much or too little, or is waiting for work because of bottlenecks elsewhere in the team.
- Re-prioritise daily, to ensure the team meets their own and the company goals.
- Re-allocate work if someone is off sick or on holiday
- Solve problems as and when they arise, such as shortage of materials, changing customer requirements, IT issues, staff shortages, changing management priorities, or new product or service requirements.
- Make decisions when incidents occur outside the scope of the team's roles.
- Ensure you record and action basic HR issues quickly and accurately, such as pay, overtime, sick pay, holidays, compassionate leave requests and flexible working requests.

- Monitor the performance of the team and individuals, so you are confident everyone is pulling their weight and delivering their share of the work.
- Give feedback to team members to motivate them and help them to improve.
- Complete formal procedures such as appraisals and objective setting to company timescales.
- Coach and develop team members to improve their skills, knowledge, and ability.
- Keep records of conversations and meetings, as well as the processes mentioned above, so that you have evidence of what was said and agreed. This may be useful if a team member applies for promotion, asks for a reference, or stops performing to their usual level.

The thing about each of these team needs, is that quite often your team can't do their job until you have done your part.

If you don't allocate work to them each day, they won't have enough to do. If you don't know who is busy and who isn't, you won't be able to move work around the team to maximise what the team can deliver.

You won't know who needs more work and who needs less. Who has time to learn a new task that might ease the workload for someone else in the team?

If you aren't monitoring individual performance, you won't know whether the person who is busy is delivering as much as the person who appears not to have enough to do, or is in fact achieving less each day, while the apparently unbusy person is calmly and effectively doing their work much more efficiently.

And if you don't give feedback to the team, nothing will change, nothing will improve, and people will wonder and discuss between them why you haven't appeared to notice how busy or not they are.

As a manager – a good manager – your first priority is understanding exactly how each member of your team is performing, and your second is to remove any blocks, obstacles or problems that are stopping them from performing even better.

Your third priority is efficiency.

Organisations become profitable when their income exceeds their costs. Salaries are often the highest expense for a business, and it makes sense to consider salary costs when you look at the workload on your management desk.

If you have a report to write, is it sensible for the organisation to pay your salary to produce the report, or is it likely to be more cost effective for a member of your team, on a lower salary, to produce that report?

If your salary is £16 per hour as a manager, and it would take you an hour to write the report, but your employee (on £12 per hour) could also write it in an hour, then – on cost alone – it's better value for the company if the employee writes the report.

Think carefully about what you can delegate to your team. Tasks that they might enjoy doing, or which might help to develop them, or which link to other tasks they already do and might enrich their current role. You don't have to do everything yourself, and moving work around the team to find the most cost-effective way of doing it should include the work that sits on your desk too.

You are the judge, jury (and executioner)

If you're a parent with more than one child, you'll probably have more mediation and conflict handling skills than you realise.

As a manager, those skills are going to be extremely useful.

Teams argue and disagree. People misunderstand instructions or team decisions. Some people are constantly on the look-out for opportunities to catch others out.

And some people are natural victims. Colleagues talk over them, ignore them, or just don't listen to them.

Conflict is natural whenever people work together. To some degree it is healthy for a team to have things they disagree about. It's good for people to air their concerns or their fears, and for others to consider these carefully before reaching a decision.

So don't feel the need to wade in every time there is a bit of upset in the team. Pick your battles wisely. You don't have to get involved in every dispute. Teams can often work problems out for themselves without your involvement. But be on the lookout for signs you do need to intervene. For example, where team members can't resolve their issues in a healthy and fair way, or treat certain individuals unfairly or unreasonably.

Be mindful of whether the same people win every argument, and whether that is healthy for the team.

Be ready to intervene if there are any signs of bullying or victimisation.

And be prepared to be unpopular, because if you intervene, you are going to have to decide on the issue the team are arguing about.

You are the manager after all. The buck stops with you.

I've talked quite generally so far about why managers matter, the common myths about management, and what changes when you become a manager. And you can already see that management is a complex job.

So, what can you do, as a new manager, to prepare yourself, and help yourself to be a more effective leader and manager of people?

Understanding the context you are working in is critical. Over the next few chapters, we are going to look at how well you know yourself, your business, and your team, and how knowing each of these better will help you to be a more effective manager.

CHAPTER 4
KNOW YOURSELF

Management is a role. Like being a partner, or a parent, or a sibling, it is a role with some rules and expectations that come with the job.

And like parents, or partners, or siblings, there is room for lots of different types of managers. Some managers are more successful in certain situations or with certain personality types. You can see this amongst football managers, who may be very successful in one club, but then fail to replicate their achievements when they move to a different club.

Understanding who you are, and what you stand for, is key to helping you recognise how your strengths will help you in some situations and with some people. Of course, the reverse is also true; your strengths and weaknesses might make life difficult for you (and for those you manage) at other times.

So, spend some time on this chapter. It really is a critical part of your journey into management, and thinking hard about what makes you tick and what you are good at, and not so good at, is going to pay dividends for you as a team manager.

What made you the person you are today?

What are the life and career events that have brought you to this management role that you are in today?

Who shaped you? Was it a family member who inspired you to behave in a certain way? Was it a teacher who changed your outlook on life? Was there someone who made you think, "Whatever I do in life, I don't want to be like them"?

We're all a product of our history. Every experience you have ever had, every person you have ever met, and every decision you have ever made, has brought you to this point today. Even picking up this book was a decision, born out of your own personal history and experience. We are shaped by the events that have happened to us, the people we have met along the way, managers and co-workers we have spent time with, friends, family members, partners, and children.

Those experiences equip us with values, strengths, knowledge, skills, and attitudes.

They also give us some emotional baggage, which can be triggered in ways we don't always understand.

And the thing is, everyone that works for you, in your team, comes with their own history, values, skills and emotional baggage too. When yours and theirs are similar, you probably feel that you understand what makes them tick. When you encounter people whose values you don't understand, who seem to get upset at the strangest things, or who just don't seem motivated to want to do things the way you do them, it can be more difficult to build a successful relationship. That doesn't make them a difficult person, but it does mean they are different and you will need to invest time in understanding just what it is that inspires and stimulates them to do the things they do.

So many of the issues that you will encounter at work are a result of the differences between you and others. So often we think we understand other people because we know what we think or feel, and therefore we assume that is what they think and feel. Although you may have realised, while reading that sentence, just how nonsensical that assumption is.

Just as we all have unique histories, unique experiences, unique personalities, and unique skillsets, we are all unique people who will react uniquely to different events and conversations.

That is the beauty of people. That is the challenge of team management!

Do you know your own values?

It is worth spending a bit of time thinking about your own personal values. They drive more of your behaviour than you probably realise, and affect how you perceive other people. When values are aligned at work, everything is easier, but if you find yourself unable to understand why a team member is behaving in a particular way, it might just be that they have very different values to yours.

Knowing your own values will help you to decide what kind of manager you are going to be, what is important to you (and therefore to your team members) and what is likely to be challenging for you as a new manager.

Many people find it difficult to articulate their own personal values. Perhaps you haven't ever thought about the inner values that drive you. So here is an exercise that can help you pinpoint what your most important values are.

Exercise:

Take a pen and a notebook, and spend a few minutes thinking about the following question.

What are your three most important values, that you uphold in every part of your life?

If nothing immediately jumps out, (or lots of things do and you can't choose) try this activity.

On the next page there is a list of 100 values. Pick 10 or 15 values from this list that are important to you. You can add other values to this list if the word you are looking for isn't here. There are no right or wrong values – only yours.

Now that you have 10 – 15 values, try to cut the list in half, keeping the values that really, really matter and you couldn't be without.

Finally try to pick 3 that seem more important than all the others. Perhaps you can think of examples to go with each of the 3 values you have chosen, or maybe they will just feel, or sound, right to you.

Achievement	*Adventure*	*Ambition*
Authority	*Autonomy*	*Balance*
Beauty	*Boldness*	*Bravery*
Challenge	*Charity*	*Community*
Compassion	*Competence*	*Connection*
Cooperation	*Creativity*	*Curiosity*
Determination	*Discipline*	*Enjoyment*
Equality	*Ethical*	*Excellence*
Fairness	*Family*	*Freedom*
Friendship	*Fun*	*Generosity*
Gratitude	*Growth*	*Happiness*
Hard work	*Honesty*	*Honour*
Humour	*Independence*	*Individuality*
Influence	*Integrity*	*Justice*
Kindness	*Knowledge*	*Leadership*
Learning	*Liberty*	*Love*
Loyalty	*Mastery*	*Meaning*
Openness	*Optimism*	*Order*
Organisation	*Originality*	*Passion*
Patience	*Peace*	**Performance**
Persistence	*Playfulness*	*Pleasure*
Popularity	*Power*	*Productivity*
Professionalism	*Purpose*	*Quality*
Reason	*Recognition*	*Religion*
Reputation	*Responsibility*	*Security*
Self-reliance	*Sensitivity*	*Service*
Sharing	*Simplicity*	*Sincerity*
Solitude	*Spirituality*	*Spontaneity*
Stability	*Status*	*Strength*
Structure	*Success*	*Support*
Sustainability	*Tolerance*	*Traditional*
Tranquillity	*Transparency*	*Trustworthiness*
Understanding	*Wealth*	*Willingness*
Wisdom		

Most people find this a really challenging exercise. Some values seem very similar but have nuances that make them different. You may find it difficult to find as many as 15 words. Or it may be really challenging to cut down your list to three.

One way of cutting down the list would be to take two values, and ask this question. If I could only have one of these until the day I die, which one would it be?

For example, would you rather have your family with you, but be poor until you die, or would you prefer to have wealth until you die, but no family around you?

Keep pairing the values and asking the same question until you get down to 3 core values.

Another clue to understanding your core personal values is to observe your own behaviour over the next few days or weeks. Often when we get particularly frustrated or angry at work, it is because one of our values is being challenged. I remember being chastised by a manager because a particular piece of work hadn't been completed while the manager was on holiday. At no point did the manager ask why the work wasn't done, and I wasn't given any opportunity to explain. I was just told – very loudly, in a public office, and several times over – that it was unacceptable for my boss to come back from holiday and find a task not completed.

I got upset – very upset. I felt unfairly treated. We'd had an absurdly busy week trying to cover the workload while the manager was away. The manager had known before they went away on holiday that it was going to be busy, but hadn't arranged any additional support. And the unfinished work wasn't even my responsibility. It wasn't handed over to me to be completed – the paperwork was hidden away where no-one would think to look for it.

Apparently, I should have known about it.

I'd even worked extra, unpaid overtime that week to make sure I had completed all the work I was responsible for. I thought I would be thanked for my commitment. Instead, I was roundly castigated.

The manager didn't even bother to ask what went wrong before launching into their own onslaught.

I still can't talk about it without ranting. As you can probably tell!

Why did I get upset? My values of fairness and integrity were being challenged. Fairness, in that I felt the manager should have asked for my side of the story before launching into a personal attack, and integrity because I felt I had done everything I was asked to do, this extra task came up on the final day of the manager's holiday, and there was no way I could have known before then that it needed doing, because the person responsible for it had hidden it away.

And that was the moment I knew I had to leave that job.

You might have a similarly dramatic moment, and such a strong feeling, that you couldn't really explain. Those strong emotions are often a sign that our values are being challenged. So, think about the times you might have felt (or been told) you were over-reacting, or couldn't understand why you became upset, or angry, or frustrated about something, and think about what values were being ignored, or undermined, or challenged through that experience. They are probably your strongest and most important values.

Why knowing your own values is so important

Our values have a powerful influence over our behaviour.

I've described above how, when our values are challenged, we can feel a strong emotional reaction.

When we are working in a role which is aligned with our values, we feel at ease. We make decisions in our roles which fit with our own personal values, as well as those of the business. We feel we are behaving authentically, doing the right thing, being true to ourselves.

If you find yourself working in an organisation with different values to your own, you will feel very differently. Every time you make a decision, in the pit of your stomach you will feel a negative reaction. Every time your manager asks you to do something that is in line with the organisation's values, yet in conflict with your own, you will feel a negative reaction inside you. You might not know why, but that reaction might be irritation, annoyance, resentment, unease, guilt, or some other sign of distress.

As a business owner, you might find yourself putting off decisions because the outcomes are out of line with your values. You might know logically that you need to restructure your business, and yet the thought of telling your team members that some of them are to lose their jobs is too difficult to contemplate. Your values of loyalty and commitment are being challenged.

After making these decisions which challenge your own values, the negative feelings might strengthen, or they might be replaced with a sort of numbness that you cannot quite describe. You may look at yourself one day and wonder when you changed, and why you are so different to the person you used to be. You might dislike yourself for some of the things you find yourself doing. Perhaps you will start to experience trouble switching off from work, or problems sleeping at night.

What you are experiencing could be anxiety, or stress. Those feelings are your body's way of telling you that you are in the wrong place, the wrong organisation, or the wrong role.

If you are the leader of your organisation, you have a choice now to change the way the organisation operates so that it is more congruent with your personal beliefs. But if you are an employed manager, you have a more difficult decision to make. Do you stay and try and change the organisation from inside your team, or do you have to leave and find something more in line with your personal values and beliefs?

A change of manager often brings with it a change in the most prominent values within an organisation. You often find that around 3-6 months after a new manager starts their role, key employees will resign and move on to other companies. People who, perhaps, have been with the organisation since it first began, will suddenly decide they have had enough – the time has come for them to move on, as the place just doesn't seem the same anymore. Long-serving employees will decide they can no longer work there.

It's a natural reaction to a change of manager. People join an organisation because they think it fits with their career path and their personal values, and it offers them a level of security and a range of working benefits that they value. When a new manager arrives, with a different approach and a different set of values, people must reassess whether they are still getting the same "deal" that they signed up to. There may have been particular characteristics or priorities their previous manager displayed that drew the employee to that manager, or made them enjoy coming to work. Change the manager and the dynamic changes. Employees have the right to decide whether it is still for them or not. Don't be surprised if it happens to you, and don't take it personally. It's just how it goes.

What motivates you?

As we have seen, our values are part of our core being, and they drive a lot of our behaviour and feelings at work. What motivates you as an individual is another important factor that will determine the type of manager you are to your team. We often think of motivation as something that is given to us by others, but motivation sits inside each one of us. As a manager, you may be able to create the conditions that switch on that motivation in other people, and yourself.

So let's think about what motivates you.

What matters most to you about work? Is it:

- Doing a good job?
- Being seen by others to do a good job?
- Being loyal to the company and committed to work?
- Learning all the time?
- Earning a good salary?
- The perks and benefits you have earned through your position?
- The people you work with?
- The responsibility you are given?
- The career path open to you?
- That work fits in with family life?

Rate these in order, from 1 (the most important to you) to 10 (the least important to you).

How easy or difficult was that? Did the answers surprise you?

Would you have answered any differently a year ago? Do you think your answers might change in a couple of years' time?

The truth is that your answers might change tomorrow morning! Motivation is a bit like that. It ebbs and flows, depending on what is happening in your life now. That's why you can be super-keen to work on a report one day, and can't face picking it up the next. On top of staff performance conversations this week, then forget about them for 3 months. Happy and content in your job one day, and ready to walk out at the first sign of trouble the next.

Understanding what is currently motivating you, and why, and what might happen to change that is useful in helping you to plan your time and your tasks. You may have more energy, and be more motivated, in the mornings, or at the start of the week. They would be good times to do some of your more difficult or complicated work. At other times in the week you might feel more lethargic, and find it difficult to concentrate for any length of time. These would be good times to do some more routine work, or talk with other team members if that gives you a boost of energy.

What do you think would happen if you asked your team members to rank these in order of importance to them?

Well, let me tell you what would happen...they would all come out with a different set of priorities, in a different order to you.

And something even more interesting...if you repeat the exercise in 6 months' time, you will get a whole different set of results.

We're all different. We are all motivated by different things, at different times in our lives. If an employee has just joined your organisation after being made redundant from their previous role, job security is likely to be an important motivator for them. Impressing their boss might matter too. Whereas someone working towards their retirement might enjoy the people they work with, or the way their working hours fit with their family life or hobbies. Other people at the same stage of life might be motivated by money and perks. There are no rules about what motivates people.

Your assumptions about yourself and others

Well, actually, there is one rule.

You can't make assumptions about what people are or are not going to be motivated by.

The biggest mistake most managers make is to assume everyone else in their team is like them. You worked hard to get where you are today. You volunteered for extra projects so you could gain more experience. You were committed to your own development so you spent lots of your own time reading books, researching on the internet, listening to experts on videos or podcasts. Maybe you did some further qualifications to help you in your career. You travelled when work needed you to. Stayed late. Worked evenings and weekends to keep up or get ahead. Sacrificed time that you might have spent with your family, or on hobbies, to do your job well.

To you, these are symbols of your commitment to your career and your employer.

The trouble is, other people aren't you. Their idea of commitment might be that they never took a day off sick. Or they were never late for work. Or they didn't punch their manager when that boss said something stupid. Their idea of commitment to their career might simply be that they have stuck at it through thick and thin, they don't moan about you in the pub, or that they've got you out of a hole now and again by knowing something no-one else knows.

They might not even see commitment in terms of their job – perhaps they think of commitment in terms of their family? Or meeting their mortgage payments. Or being able to afford to socialise with friends.

Does that make them less valuable as employees?

Maybe, but you know, I don't think it does. If every employee wanted to climb the corporate ladder like you have, you'd have a lot of disgruntled employees to work with, because there simply aren't enough jobs for people to aspire to in most organisations. For the sake of continuity, it's helpful to have some people in your team who are just happy to do what they do. They come to work every day, they do what they are employed to do, and then they go home. They don't want to progress within the organisation. They just want to come in, work their hours, and leave on time. And there's nothing wrong with that.

In fact, Jack Welch, Business Guru and CEO of GEC said that in most workplaces, about 20% of your employees will be high fliers, 70% will do OK, and 10% probably need to leave. If you spend your working life trying to turn the 70% into high fliers, you will devote a huge amount of time and effort to something that isn't going to happen. Better to focus on identifying and developing the 20%, and doing what you need to do to move the 10% along to a more suitable organisation.

Before you dust off the disciplinary or capability procedures, though, I want you to spend some time thinking about the assumptions that you make about people in your team.

- Who do you think is loyal and committed to their work?
- Who is your best worker?
- Who would work extra hours if you asked them?
- Who is lazy and underperforming?
- Who is argumentative?
- Who needs to leave the team?

Now stop and ask yourself why you think these things. What proof do you have that these assumptions are true?

No, don't just skip past that question. Stop and really think for a few minutes.

- What is it that makes you assume your best worker is your best worker?
- What *measures* are you using to make that judgement?
- What *proof* do you have that performance really is at the level you say it is? Real proof? The "stand up in court and prove it" level of proof?
- What do you have to *tolerate* from your "best worker" to get that level of performance from them?

No one is perfect. And quite often the best performer in a team isn't great at everything. We all have some weaknesses (or "development areas") and your best performer is no exception.

I know of teams where the best salesperson is streets ahead of the rest of the team in orders taken, although his administration is so shocking that orders don't get processed within the agreed timescales, quotes are often inaccurate, and as well as having no friends in the sales admin team, he also generates the highest number of complaints from customers.

Or project leaders who always deliver on time and within budget, only by making the lives of the rest of the project team a complete misery for the whole duration of the project. They might have the highest turnover of staff, but because they always deliver on time and in budget, the staffing issues are tolerated.

Or teams where there is someone who never communicates with the rest of the team, but they are the only one who knows how to operate a certain piece of software or kit. The company is missing out on business because they aren't passing on messages, yet no-one dares to tackle the team member because if they take offence and leave, the business can't continue to function.

Now, you might be thinking that you would never allow yourself to get into such a ludicrous situation where you are effectively held hostage by an employee who is demonstrating such undesirable behaviours. Nevertheless, I bet there is someone in your organisation doing just that.

As an HR Consultant and a Management Coach, I have seen so many companies where there are clear performance issues with an individual, yet no-one will tackle the situation for fear of losing the employee or upsetting them.

Just stop it. Stop it right now. If your team or your business has someone like this within it, they are not your best worker. Not by any stretch of the imagination. They might look like a knight in shining armour, riding to the rescue of your sales targets, but look at the chaos they leave in their wake. Show me a team with an untouchable employee who is best at something the organisation values, and I'll show you at least 30% of that team who are actively looking for another job. And 30% who are seriously considering starting to look.

Before we leave this subject, let's have a look at the laziest person in your team.

Again, think about what evidence you have to back up this assumption.

People may be labelled as lazy because they don't get to work on time in the mornings. And in certain environments this can be pretty frustrating, particularly in a customer-facing role, or where that individual is responsible for opening up the premises in the morning so that everyone else can get into work.

However, getting to work for a certain time of day isn't really life or death for most businesses. And that person who is "lazy" might have spent 3 hours already this morning getting their children dressed, fed, and dropped off at various nurseries, childminders, or schools. They may be caring for an older relative who they must help get out of bed in the morning and make sure they are washed, fed, and have taken their medication. They may themselves be taking medication that makes it difficult for them to get going in the mornings. They might just not go to bed on time.

The thing is, until you know what is going on in their lives, you can't possibly give them a label of "lazy".

"Ah", you say, "I see them sitting at their desk during the day, doing nothing, gazing into space. Therefore, none of the above excuses apply – they are just lazy."

OK, but before you can say for certain they are lazy, let's ask a few more questions.

- Why have they stopped working (if they have stopped, that is)?
- Is their computer old and slow, and they must wait for things to load up?
- Are they due to see a client, make a call, or start a task in a couple of minutes' time?
- Have they encountered an issue they need to think how to deal with?
- Do they have enough work to do?
- Do they know how to do the work they have to do? (Are you sure about that?)
- Do they have too much work to do and no idea where to start or what to prioritise?
- Were they working 10 minutes ago and are just taking a short break from their screen?
- Have they just received some bad news?

Now your person may be genuinely lazy. Equally, you might be making assumptions about their behaviour before you have enough information to prove your assumptions are true.

As a manager you are being paid to make quick decisions, yet people's behaviour isn't something you can decide about quickly. You need to make time to understand your team members, what is going on in their lives, and what makes them tick.

You also need to be objective about individual performance. You need to see both the good and the not so good, the positive and the negative. You need, in short, to see people for what they are. Whole people, with their own unique interests, strengths, challenges, flaws, and limitations. Whole people with lives, for which work is a part, but only a part. You employ them for the hours it states in their contract of employment, and you must understand that what happens in the rest of their week will sometimes come to work with them. So, make a vow to yourself that whenever you feel an assumption appearing in your mind about one of your team, you will stop, and ask yourself:

- What evidence is there, really, to support this assumption?
- What else could be happening at work for this team member that has triggered this assumption?
- What could be happening at home for this team member that might have an impact on this situation?
- And perhaps the hardest question of all. What is going on for you, as the manager, at work or at home, that might be making you react as you have to someone's behaviour?

What are your strengths?

What are the things you are good at? And not just good, but better than just about anyone you know or have ever worked with?

We all have something we do that is special. That only we can do, or that only we can do the way we do it. Honed over many years of experience, practiced in many different environments, or just something we enjoy doing so much it never really feels like work.

The thing about our strengths is that we probably underestimate them, because we find them so easy to do. It just doesn't seem right to claim something as a strength that we can do in our sleep. In fact, because we can do it without thinking, we can be guilty of forgetting just how much effort we have put into learning our craft over our lifetimes.

My youngest daughter is a trampolinist. She started learning when she was eight years old, just as most children learn. Bouncing up and down, the odd seat drop and half twist. And gradually, over the years, she has learnt new moves, perfected them, and built further new techniques on top of old ones. She now speaks a language I don't understand, peppered with words and phrases I can't decipher, like Rudi, lazy back Cody and one and three barani ball out, the last one conjuring up - for me - a picture of a biryani curry every time she says it.

I prefer to watch recorded versions of her competitive performances because I know she has got through them unscathed. She can perform double back somersaults (jumping up and turning two somersaults before landing). She performs at elite level in national competitions. And at those competitions she usually finishes in the top third of the entries. She will talk about how others are better at trampolining, what she needs to do to improve, and be wishing she could perform a move as well as another competitor.

She forgets how amazing a trampolinist she is, because she doesn't give herself credit for the great things she can do. She is always looking for the gap, for the next person above her, for the skills she needs to improve.

And as managers it is very easy to fall into that trap too. To focus on the things you don't think you do well, while forgetting the areas where you outperform most of your colleagues.

Exercise:

Take a big sheet of paper, and start writing. List everything you know you do well. Remember to include things you don't enjoy doing, as well as the things you love (although it's likely you will enjoy doing most of the things you are good at).

If you start to run out of ideas, think about the things your colleagues would come and ask you for help with, and write those down. The things others would call you an expert in, even if you don't necessarily agree with them yourself.

Refer to your appraisals, promotion feedback, correspondence from customers, colleagues, other managers, or team members. Look for examples where you have been thanked for solving a problem or achieving a result.

When you genuinely can't think of any more work examples, think about your home life. What do you do in your spare time? What hobbies do you currently have? What were your previous hobbies? What problems do you love solving at home, and what problems do others ask you to solve for them? Keep writing, and don't stop until that page is full.

What are your weaknesses?

Let's be honest, most of us will find this question much easier and probably more comfortable to answer. We are often more painfully aware of our weaknesses – the things we know we can't do as well as other people. The areas we fall short in within our current roles.

Exercise:

On a different sheet of paper, write down your perceived weaknesses (or development areas if you prefer).

Think about your work in terms of managing yourself, managing the team, and managing the task. List the areas you know need some work from you to get right.

When you have the lists of your strengths and weaknesses, I want you to look carefully at them.

Starting with your strengths, circle the strengths that you get to use every day in your current job.

Now, with a different coloured pen or pencil, circle the strengths that you get to use every week in your current job.

And with a third colour, circle the strengths that you use at least once a month in your current job.

Then turn to your weaknesses, and repeat the exercise.

Circle the weaknesses that your job exposes every day of the week

In a different colour, circle the weaknesses that your job exposes at least once a week.

And in a third colour, circle any weaknesses that your job exposes once a month.

Now look at your two pieces of paper and ask yourself this.

What proportion of your strengths and weaknesses have you circled?

Ideally you will have circled more than half your strengths, and fewer than half your weaknesses. That means your job plays to your strengths, and doesn't expose too many of your weaknesses, meaning you probably feel happy and fulfilled at work most of the time.

However, if you have circled fewer than half your strengths, and/or more than half of your weaknesses, you have a tough question to answer.

Why are you doing this job?

Really, really think about this. If you are in a job that isn't playing to your strengths, are you ever going to be really happy or satisfied in this role? And if, day in day out, you are doing work that exposes more of your weaknesses than your strengths, can you ever feel happy that you are giving of your best at work?

Because you know something? You are really going to struggle to turn your weaknesses into strengths. It is possible, but it takes time, energy, and lots and lots of effort. You probably hate most of the things on your weaknesses list, so even if you could improve the skills, you would probably hate the experience of doing it. By contrast, developing your strengths is a walk in the park. Because working with our strengths is easy and fun, we are more likely to be motivated to find ways of improving the way we do them.

The truth is this. If you are in a job that doesn't play to your strengths, you are going to spend most of your time stressed, tired, and unhappy. You will constantly be aware of the gap between what the job needs, and what you are able to give to the role. You will always be looking over your shoulder at others who can do the job better than you can do it (in your eyes at least). You will feel insecure, threatened, and miserable. And you will take most of those feelings home with you to share with your family.

You need a role that uses lots of your strengths most of the time, and lets you develop a few of your weaknesses at the same time. That way you will feel challenged and inspired, and will see the improvement in your skills as you go.

What does success look like, for you?

We all have different ideas of what it means to be successful. For some people it might be to own or drive a particular car, or live in a certain area. Others might aspire to a second home, holidays abroad, time for hobbies. You may already have a wish list of your own, or a vision board. These material symbols of success can be strong motivators for some people.

We don't often think consciously about what success in a particular job might look like. It is worth taking the time to do this, because management is a multi-faceted role, and it's very easy to spend your time dwelling on the things that aren't going so well. Sadly, it is still rare in business to be given feedback on the things you are good at.

Here is a quick activity you could try.

Take an A4 sheet of paper and draw a big + sign to divide the sheet into 4 sections.

Label the sections as follows.

See	*Hear*
Feel	*Think*

Then, in the middle of the sheet, write the following words. "When I am a successful team manager, I will…"

Now write in the first section what you will see when you are a successful team manager. For example, you might see your team working out a problem together, without involving you. Or you may see team members being promoted into management roles because you have developed them so well. Write as many examples as you can think of, before you move on.

In the next section, write down what you will hear when you are a successful manager. Perhaps you will hear lots of compliments about your team's performance? Or maybe you will hear cheers around the office as your team smash their targets? Again, keep writing until you have no more ideas.

In the next two sections you are going to explore what you will be feeling and thinking when you are successful. Will the feeling be pride? Contentment? Confidence? Anticipation? You'll probably imagine several feelings, so write them all down, even if some contradict others.

And finally, what will you be thinking when you are a successful manager? Maybe it will be "I've got this" or "Where's my next job?" or even "This actually feels quite easy now"? Write down every thought.

And now put your piece of paper away somewhere safe. The back of your diary would be good (if you have a paper diary). Or maybe you could tuck it away inside your purse or wallet. Keep it somewhere you can find it easily, and get it out from time to time. Maybe when you are having a good day, or perhaps even a bad day. You might find that you are seeing, hearing, thinking, or feeling things that you associate with success, even when you think other aspects of the job aren't going so well. And you may also realise that success as a manager isn't necessarily about the next promotion or pay increase. It's more often the smile on an employee's face when they achieve something, or the pride you feel when your manager notices improvements in your team, or the present your team club together and buy for you.

Do you have the temperament to be a manager?

You are going to face all sorts of issues as a manager. So many different situations that you will come to believe are being deliberately manipulated in order to wind you up, or just be plain difficult.

As an HR professional, I am fortunate to be one step removed from the day-to-day issues that arise between managers and their teams. And distance gives a very different perspective to some of these flashpoints. That is not to say that no employee ever means to be difficult or obstructive. Or that every manager is right on every occasion. Neither of those two are true. There are two sides to every story – and a third if someone outside the manager-employee relationship observes the situation. Let's look at some examples.

Someone questions your authority

If you're particularly inexperienced as a manager, this is likely to be a hot button for you. Your own lack of confidence – which is fine, by the way, because you are new and learning a job for the first time – is likely to lead to an immediate, intense reaction for you.

How dare they question an instruction or an order?

But, the ability to accept a challenge from another employee as a valid, yet different, point of view, is a sign of strength.

Employees challenge their managers for all sorts of reasons. These can include:

Fear - they really think you are going to make a big mistake that will have implications for them, or they believe your decision will have a negative impact on their personal or professional life.

They don't think you really mean it – if you've ever watched a baby crawling towards a fire or trying to poke something into an electric socket, and heard the parent cry "No" you will know that the next step is for the baby to try again. They need to test how firm the boundaries really are, and psychologists tell us that babies who know exactly where their boundaries are feel a lot more secure than babies who are not so closely parented. I don't think we ever really lose that need to test boundaries. We see it in school children and teenagers, who constantly want to overreach what their parents believe is appropriate. And we see it in the workplace too. We all do it from time to time – it's human nature.

They are working from different information – this is a common reason for conflict at work, and one that many managers overlook. It's easy to assume everyone sees things the way you do, and everyone knows the information you are working from. But sometimes your employees are missing some vital information. Sometimes they know more than the manager. Remember when you communicate a decision to your team you may have to explain exactly what you know, and how you have used that knowledge to reach your conclusion on the way forward.

You're wrong – Let's be honest, it's going to happen. A lot. Your employees have a personal stake in the way the team and the business operate. Their homes, families, financial security, and social standing are dependent upon your business being successful. So, if they believe you are wrong, and they tell you, listen and be prepared to reconsider. The more emotionally intense their reaction is, the more you need to listen to really understand what is driving their disagreement.

Employees want and need to be able to trust their manager. They need to test your decisions and see if you really mean it. It will take them a while with a new manager to really understand you and learn to trust you. And that trust might come from seeing you not jump to decisions before you have full information, or standing firm when you know you are right, and when they know you will change your mind when you are given new information that proves your original decision is wrong.

Someone breaks a rule

It's easy to jump to the conclusion that they did it deliberately, they knew they were doing wrong, and they deserve to be punished. Nevertheless, before you make that jump, ask yourself whether you can really be sure they knew the rule, and therefore that they were doing wrong.

When were they told about the rule? Did you hear from their own mouth that they understood what that rule meant, and that it applied to them? Quite often we think we have told people what is expected, only to discover that they didn't hear, or were distracted and not really listening, or they heard part of the instruction and were thinking about that and not really paying attention to the rest of the talk.

Maybe you have written the instruction down – although even then, people don't always interpret what they read in the same way as the writer intended. Some people don't read well, some don't have English as a first language, sometimes the grammar and punctuation changes the meaning of the sentence.

And if you only say a rule once, you might as well save your breath. People need to hear it repeatedly for it to really sink in. And if you don't repeat it, or you stop reminding them of the rule, it's understandable if your team assume that means the rule no longer applies.

The only way you can be sure that your team have understood rules or instructions is by asking them to explain the rules to you. And even then, you will need to constantly re-brief rules and instructions so that people don't forget.

Someone is late

We can all make mistakes sometimes. Alarms don't go off. Cars really can be difficult to start, or have flat tyres. An accident can hold traffic up. Children can play up or nurseries need a word before the parent can leave the child with them. But when you hear the same excuses from the same employee repeatedly, it's easy to jump to the conclusion that they aren't taking ownership of the problem, and that they are being late deliberately.

If the employee has always been late, think about whether anyone has ever told them the rules about timekeeping. Are you sure? How many times have they sidled in late and no-one has said anything? Maybe they have drawn the conclusion that timekeeping isn't something the company is too worried about?

If lateness is a recent pattern, you need to understand what has changed for the employee. Perhaps in their personal life – a change of nursery or school for their child? A different route to work because of roadworks? A change to bus or train timetables? An elderly dependent suddenly relying on them for care? Or maybe an illness or medical condition that is worse in the mornings? Talking to your employees regularly and understanding what is happening in their life outside work may transform the way you think about their timekeeping and change your mind about what action – if any – is necessary.

Of course, sometimes the employee is just playing games with you. Or they have a real issue getting out of bed in the morning because they are partying too late at night. Some people hit the snooze button more times than they should, or don't charge their phones up at night, so the alarm doesn't go off in the morning.

Unless you spend time with your employee and speak to them before you decide on the action to be taken, you will never know the right way to tackle a problem such as lateness.

Someone doesn't want to engage in learning and development

Not everyone is going to be a high flier – and let's face it, no organisation could possibly promote everyone to a management role. So, if you have team members who are happy to come to work and do the job they are paid to do, and aren't interested in progressing up the corporate ladder, then that is a good thing. We need some team members to stay in their roles and use their experience to help new members learn the ropes. Pushing those people to apply for promotion to roles they don't want isn't going to be good for the employee, or the organisation.

Then again, opting out of ALL learning and development is a different matter entirely. Jobs change over time. Even a job that keeps the same title and does essentially the same work can expect some changes. Systems evolve. Technology changes. Departments are reorganised and new work becomes part of existing roles. So, your employees need to understand that while it's fine for them not to want promotion, there will always be an element of job-related training that is essential for them to complete in order to stay on top of the job.

And you, as a manager, need to make sure people are learning and developing every year. The ability to learn, to take in new information and to change the way we perform a task as a result – is a skill. And if people get out of the habit of learning and developing their skills, they will forget how to do it. Learning will become difficult for them, something to be avoided. Their skills will stagnate and decline, and they won't be able to keep up with the challenges of the job. Eventually you will find yourself with a team that is unable to cope with the requirements the business places on them. They will become redundant, not, necessarily, through choice, more because you as their manager did not equip them with the knowledge and skills needed to continue doing their jobs in the longer term. The responsibility for your team's destiny sits on your shoulders. Use it wisely.

Someone goes to your boss to complain about you
There is a saying that you can please some of the people all the time, and you can please all the people some of the time. But you cannot please all the people all the time.

And even the very best managers, the most competent, the most knowledgeable, and the most emotionally intelligent leaders, will find themselves in situations where a team member takes such exception to what they have said or done that the team member will go above their head and complain to their boss about the manager.

So, if you are new to the role and inexperienced, and this happens to you, see it for what it is. Someone is trying to find the boundaries. They are seeking to gain some allies and have life revert to what it was before you came along.

Expect your manager to give them the time to vent. Good managers listen to what their team members have to say. Expect that you will be asked to give your side of events. Fair managers will make sure they have all the facts before they make a decision.

Understand that these actions are not your manager siding with the team member. This is how good managers resolve conflict – by listening to both sides and drawing their own conclusion about where the truth falls between the two of you.

Expect your manager to either take your side, or coach you on what happened, and what you could do differently next time. And whatever you do, don't take it personally. Learn from the experience, understand what led to the individual going to your manager, and work out how to avoid it happening again.

You're asked to do something you don't agree with

This, I'm afraid, is part of management life. You will be given information that you cannot share with your team. You will be involved in plans for your team or the business that you may not agree with, and you may be asked to communicate those plans to your team.

You may feel that honesty is the best policy. That you need to share the information you have been given, or your doubts about the direction of the business, with your team. You may feel this will help to demonstrate your integrity.

I have grave doubts about this approach. In my experience, teams want to have confidence in their manager, and believe that the organisation is doing the right thing. That makes them feel safe. The organisation (assuming you work for someone else) also wants to have confidence that you are on the side of the business and will do all you can to help the business achieve its goals. It's what they pay you for, after all. So while, in certain organisational cultures, and with certain personalities, a degree of brutal honesty can work to bring people onside, in most businesses it does not. And in those organisations, publicly admitting doubts about the organisation's decisions or directions is likely to be seriously career-limiting for a manager.

I recommend sticking to the golden rule of management. You can say whatever you truly think behind closed doors, to your manager's face. You can disagree, stamp your feet, present alternative ideas, or threaten to resign if you really feel that strongly.

But the minute that door opens, and you come face-to-face with your team, you must own that decision that you violently disagree with as if you made it yourself. You cannot allow your team to see a flicker of uncertainty or opposition. In government it is called Cabinet collective responsibility, and it applies equally in business.

We've covered a lot in this chapter. Don't jump ahead yet. Go back and complete all the exercises. They really will help you to understand yourself better, and have a clearer picture of why you get on well with some team members and not with others, or why you find some situations more challenging than others. We're going to move on in the next chapter to think about the organisation you work in – so make sure you know yourself first.

CHAPTER 5
KNOW YOUR BUSINESS

I f managers and employees are to make the right choices, choose the right priorities to work on, and behave in the right way, they need to have a clear understanding of what the business stands for and what it expects of its people.

Without that understanding, they are likely to make decisions that don't sit well with the company culture, or don't help the organisation to achieve its targets.

Having a mission, vision and values statement is a useful way of communicating to employees and managers the type of organisation they are working for, and how they are expected to behave.

Let's have a quick look at the context of a business, and understand what is meant by a mission, a vision, and organisational values.

Your business and the world it's in

What's happening outside your business, out there in the big, wide world?

It's quite easy to get so absorbed in what is going on inside your business that you forget to look at what is going on in the wider economy, in the political world, or internationally. You can almost believe that the outside world doesn't matter when you are working inside a business. But since 2020 organisations in the UK have had to prepare for and deal with the consequences of Brexit, which has changed the way we trade with the EU, and a global pandemic which has changed the way we work, our social interactions and our feelings of safety and security.

Even in more normal times, the outside world can have a big impact on what you can do inside a business, including the type of culture your business has, and the behaviours that managers and employees are likely to demonstrate inside the organisation.

If you are operating in a private sector business during an economic boom, you may have finance readily available to help businesses invest for growth, and a government that supports business and tries to cut red tape wherever it can. And in this situation your organisation might find finance easy to obtain, customers lining up to buy your products or services, and employees eager to join your successful organisation. If money is plentiful, there will be lots of opportunities to invest in the business, improve the way people work, train employees, and help people progress in their careers. People will enjoy working for an organisation at a time like this, because while there may be pressure to work hard, it is likely employees will be well rewarded for their efforts.

By contrast, if that same private sector business finds itself operating in a recession, with a government that favours public sector provision over the private sector, with high taxes and lots of legislation to protect consumers and employees, the situation will look very different.

Vacancies might go unfilled as a way of saving money, putting pressure on employees to take on more work. Training and expenses budgets are likely to be cut, removing opportunities for people to grow and develop their skills. Equipment won't be replaced, so it will break down more often, piling more pressure on employees already struggling to meet increased targets. And salaries are likely to be frozen, or other benefits cut, as the business tries to reduce its costs wherever it can.

There are other factors which might make life easier or more difficult for your organisation, and which may also affect the mindset of the employees who work for you.

You might think of politics as something that doesn't really matter too much to your life, yet the UK's relationships with other countries can affect things like the price or availability of raw materials or parts for your manufacturing process, or the way your organisation can trade with other countries. And within the UK, politicians can make laws that affect the way your business can operate, or how easy it is to recruit and dismiss employees.

Another key factor to consider outside the organisation is how people feel about your organisation, what it produces, and the way it does business. As a nation, our preferences change over time – environmental and sustainability concerns have become much more important for customers, so electric cars and green energy producers are expecting rapid growth, while companies that have a reputation for high levels of wastage or inefficient production methods are likely to lose customers.

The global pandemic, and Brexit, are blamed for a shortage of workers in hospitality, haulage, retail, and healthcare organisations. Employers in those industries are going to have to think of creative ways to cope with recruitment challenges, which might include increased wages or using new technology to reduce the number of roles needed. Both will increase costs, and neither will solve all the problems these employers have. Managing inside these organisations will be very different to how it was before 2020, and will require different management skills and behaviours.

There are lots of other ways to look at the external world, and some factors will be more important to some industries than others. The important thing to remember is that the specific factors that affect your business will have an effect – either positive, negative, or neutral – on your ability to find and keep the right employees. Consequently, they will also influence the kind of culture you can create within your team and wider organisation, and the way your employees feel about working for you.

Managing in a growing organisation which is continually reinvesting in the business, and offering opportunities for employees to work flexibly, grow and progress, is one thing.

Managing a team paid around minimum wage in an organisation fighting for its survival, where every penny of expenditure is fought over, is something else entirely.

Neither environment means you are automatically going to be a good, or a bad manager. That choice is entirely down to you. I have seen fantastic managers working in commercially challenging environments, who still manage to help their people grow and prosper. And I have seen managers in healthy, growing organisations act like mini-dictators.

The external environment is a factor that will influence the freedom and choices you have when managing your team. But it should never be an excuse for being an unreasonable manager.

Mission, vision, and values

Whether you are providing a product or a service, within the private, public, or not-for-profit sectors, a mission statement tells your employees, customers, and other stakeholders why you exist.

You might think it's obvious why you exist. You might say it's to make money, or to sell paperclips or whatever you produce. A mission statement should give an indication of who you serve, and what is different about your business to any other business that exists to make money or sell paperclips. Mission statements are typically short – up to about 15 words – and therefore to the point.

A vision statement sets out where the organisation aspires to be when it achieves its mission. It focuses on the future, and gives everyone associated with the organisation a clear direction.

Values tell employees about the behaviours, beliefs, and principles the organisation stands for. They describe the desired culture – the way you do things – and they provide guiding principles for employees about how they should behave.

The mission and vision are like the satnav for an organisation, telling you where you are, and where you are heading. The values are the compass employees can use when the satnav loses the signal, or the route is blocked and you don't know which way to go.

Taken together, the mission, vision and values tell people what the business is about, where it is going, and how it will behave on the way to achieving its mission and vision.

When your employees find themselves in a situation where there is no company policy, no precedent, and no-one to ask what to do, the mission, vision and values will guide them to make the right choice, or decision, in line with the company's culture and its reason for being.

Far from being a pointless piece of paper, your mission, vision, and values tell people whether you are the type of organisation they want to do business with, or be employed by. People who feel aligned with your mission, vision and values will enjoy working with you, feel inspired and engaged in achieving your goals because they will be in line with their personal goals. And those who don't identify with your mission, vision, and values, will clearly understand why some decisions or actions feel uncomfortable for them. They just don't believe in you.

And mission, vision and values matter when you recruit people, when you induct them, in the way you manage their performance, in how you'll respond to requests to work from home or work flexible hours. They will hugely influence the type of manager you are able to be.

Business Owners - what is going on in the deepest, darkest corners of your business?

If you are a business owner, this section is for you. How much do you really know about your organisation?

If you own the business, you probably think you know everything there is to know about it. You might even have built it from scratch yourself.

But the bigger your business becomes, the more likely it is that there are dark corners you haven't looked in for a while, where things are happening that you are not aware of!

The great challenge, as a team or organisation grows, is to keep everyone on the same path, heading for the same goal, and following the same cultural values and norms. Maintaining that common understanding of what the team and business stands for, and how it should behave in good and bad times, is critical to maintaining the credibility and trust of your customers and potential clients.

It's also difficult to do. You can't be everywhere, and you shouldn't be. Though if you are to choose the right strategy for the future, you need to know with certainty how your business operates, what it is truly good at, and where it has challenges.

And the key to knowing is the quality of the relationships you have with your team members. All of them. Whether they have the trust and confidence in you to tell you when things are going wrong, or whether they have learned to keep bad news from the boss.

You might think you know everyone in the organisation – you may even have recruited them all yourself if you own the business. But how well do you really know them now? Do you know what is going on in their personal lives? Whether they are still married? How many children they have and how old they are? Do you know if they are happy in their work, or just going through the motions? Do you know who does what, whether they are all doing work that is suited to their strengths, or how well they get on with their direct manager?

Who are the rising stars in your team or organisation? Do you have a clear career plan for them? Do you know how engaged and committed they are to the business? Do you have succession plans and contingency arrangements in place in case one of them leaves the business or is incapacitated for a significant period?

How do the teams in your business communicate with each other? Who is jostling with whom for power and control? Which of your key employees are looking for another job – or would jump ship if the opportunity arose? How do you measure team performance, and how can you be sure that your team is delivering for your business?

What decisions are people making that they believe are in line with your values, though they actually fall a long way short? Understanding the answer to this question will help you identify how well you have communicated your values – and what they really mean to you – to the rest of the team.

Alongside your mission, vision, and values, is the story of your organisation. Of how you came to exist, and what drove the founder of the business to start it and grow it. The story can give employees more clues about the type of organisation you are, and the behaviour and attitudes that will fit and be rewarded within it.

How close is the real culture of the organisation to the culture you tell everyone exists? This is one of the key questions every business owner/manager needs to ask themselves. It's very easy to write words on a values statement. However, it is the employees' lived experience while working for you that will show them the real culture of the organisation. Whether it's a "no blame" culture in which, in reality, you dare not admit to mistakes or omissions because of the consequences for your future career progression, or a "customer first" culture in which the company tries everything possible to avoid admitting fault or giving refunds. It only takes a single example of a value being undermined for employees to doubt whether the values mean anything at all. The only thing worse than no values statement, are values that don't match the behaviours and attitudes of the senior leaders in a business.

When was the last time you went and worked alongside your employees on the "shop floor"? Are you still as tuned in to the issues and challenges they face as you were when the business began?

When did you last use some of the processes your staff have to follow every day?

As organisations grow, and develop new products and services for new customers and markets, everyone must be flexible and adapt to change. Often those changes are incremental, or evolutionary, rather than transformational. In other words, little things change gradually over time. What was once a simple process can become complicated with additional steps to add something to the product or service, or communicate with another part of the business, or to meet a particular customer need. The problem comes when managers themselves become busier and busier, and don't stop to review whether processes are still as streamlined and cost-effective as they once were. It's a good idea for managers to spend time at least annually – and more often if there are significant changes to roles or processes – to walk through the system they are expecting employees to operate and check that the steps the employee now must complete all still make sense. Does this still constitute an interesting and worthwhile job for the employee? And the key question to ask yourself: *if we were starting from scratch would we have all the steps in the process that are currently there?*

Managers - how well do you know the business you work in?

If you are employed as a manager, this section is for you.

How well do you understand the business strategy your organisation is working to achieve?

Do you really know what the mission, vision and values of the organisation are? Do you fully understand what it means to operate in line with those values, what behaviours are expected, acceptable or unacceptable?

How much of the history of the business do you know about? How much does that history tell you about the culture and values of the organisation?

Who are the organisation's biggest customers? Most difficult clients? Best markets? Least profitable products or services?

What does good organisational performance look like? How close is the organisation to optimum performance? Who are the best workers in each team? Who are the guardians of the knowledge within the business? Who has the real power in the company?

Where are the bottlenecks in the organisation that prevent it from growing or improving the quality of service it provides to its customers?

What are the strengths and weaknesses of your colleagues at management level? What would it take for you to out-perform them?

What does all this mean for the way you are able to manage your team, the decisions you are permitted to make, and the control you have over the day-to-day activities of your team?

Managers and Business Owners - where is your business going?

Have you ever worked in an organisation that didn't have a business plan?

I did once. I say they didn't have a plan – they had never communicated a plan to their employees (which, from an employee's perspective, is essentially the same as not having a plan). In that organisation the impression employees shared was that the business wasn't in control of its destiny. It was like a small boat buffeted around by the waves, heading in whatever direction the wind carried it. Business seemed to "appear" rather than be sought. The organisation seemed to change priorities based on whatever customer had appeared, and employees had no idea whether they were going to have jobs in the long term, or what those jobs might look like. It would all depend on what business presented itself to the company.

Many businesses run like this, and in many respects wouldn't we all like to run a business that could afford to wait for work to arrive?

It becomes a bigger issue when you employ people. Your team need to understand where the business is going. Firstly, because they need to decide whether that is where they want to go too. It's fine being a manager or business owner who doesn't mind a bit of flexibility and good luck to drive their business's future, but your employees are stakeholders in the business and one of their fundamental needs is to feel secure about the future.

It's also difficult for employees to prioritise their workload and develop their skills if they don't understand what the business is prioritising, or what skills are likely to be needed in the future. If the business has no clear direction, then any opportunity or side-project is fair game. For the business to succeed financially, you need to ensure your employees are all focused on the same goals, and they spend all their time and energy pursuing those shared goals.

Know your role within the business

You might think you know what you are employed to do as a manager – but do you really?

Most of us have an idea, based on our job description or the discussions we have had with our manager. Even so there are often lots of details about the job that don't arise until you've spent some time working. Things that happen unexpectedly, that leave you wondering if that was something you should have acted on or made a decision about, or whether it was someone else's job to do that. Or perhaps someone in your team should have taken responsibility. Often, it's the not knowing that causes you inner stress, and the worrying about whether you are doing the right thing or not, that is the biggest problem. And the fear of asking your manager when you are thinking to yourself that you should probably already know this stuff and it's a bit late to ask.

Though if you don't ask, something happens and your manager thinks it WAS your job to act – but you didn't know so you didn't do anything, well, now you have a bigger problem. Now you are the one who is in trouble for not doing your job properly. Now your performance is going to be brought into question, your capability will be in doubt. Your job could be on the line.

So, ask the questions. Don't worry about looking foolish. Better to look foolish now, than to damage your credibility by not acting on something you should have done.

A good place to start with this is your job description.

Job descriptions are the formal documents which outline the purpose of a role, what the role holder is responsible for, and (often though not always) some of the key tasks the role holder can expect to undertake in the job.

Job descriptions tend to get a bit of a bad name in the workplace. They are often written in generic terms, which don't seem to bear much relation to what the postholder does day-to-day. And because of this, neither managers nor team members are usually bothered about keeping them up to date.

Jobs change more than you might think over the course of time; your business might have branched out into new areas of work, you might have invested in new technology and processes, and as people learn new skills, or move around the business, or leave, tasks and responsibilities are reallocated to other employees. You only need to take on 3 or 4 new responsibilities in a year for your job description to be out of date. If you haven't looked at someone's job description for a couple of years, that's 6-8 new responsibilities added, and maybe the same number removed.

And typically, what happens is this. Sarah is issued with a job description when she joins the company as an administrator. Because she is brand new to the role and the company, she knows that it will be a few weeks before the job description makes any sense to her, so she puts it away with her contract of employment, and focuses on learning the job.

Within a short while, Sarah is completely competent at the job she has been employed to do. She's also demonstrated a real talent for quickly understanding processes and being able to troubleshoot problems. She is therefore asked to write a procedure for raising invoices. Raising invoices was part of her original job description, but writing a procedure is a new task.

She does such a good job of writing the procedure, that she is given a project to systemise and write up the whole sales administration process. To make the time to do this, her responsibilities for checking and logging quotes on the sales database are given to another employee.

As is often the case, other managers have seen the great work Sarah is doing, and she is asked to help other teams to systemise the work they are doing and write up procedures.

Now she is hardly doing any sales administration work, and all her time is being spent managing projects to write up all the company's procedures. Her job description (still in the drawer with the contract of employment) bears no relation whatsoever to the work she is now doing day to day.

This becomes a problem if:

- There is any dispute over the work she is asked to do or the way she is performing the job, as the role referred to in her contract of employment is not the job she is currently undertaking.
- Her performance starts to drop – you have no current, agreed, written job description that you can manage performance against.
- You must make redundancies – she is technically still a sales administrator, so would need to be considered for redundancy against others in that team, despite the additional skills she has that might be useful elsewhere in the business.
- She leaves the company and you must replace her – but there is no current job description to recruit to.

- Her salary has been increased permanently to take account of her new responsibilities, so that it is out of line with other sales administrators if she were ever to return to that role.

- Her salary has been increased temporarily to take account of her new responsibilities, and now you no longer need her to do that work and want her to revert to her old role and lower salary. Which isn't particularly attractive to Sarah.

It's not unusual for a job description to be issued on recruitment, and then not looked at again until the individual leaves their post and the company wants to recruit a replacement. And quite often (because recruitment is all a bit of a pain and usually happens in a hurry) the same job description that was issued 5 years ago when the last postholder joined is used.

And that is a shame, because the job description is part of the contract of employment. It is the document that specifies what the job-holder is being employed to do. And if they are not doing what they are employed to do, it is the document that will be used to manage their performance, or potentially terminate their employment.

So, it is a critical document that should be kept up to date, and it should be checked with the job holder at least once a year, and any time that a new task or responsibility is added or removed, and updated as appropriate.

How to write a job description

If you don't have an up-to-date job description yourself, then you need to write one. It's not a big task, but it does take a bit of thought.

So, take a sheet of paper and – without worrying about the language and format at this stage – just jot down in bullet points the tasks you do in your job. It might help to think about the regular things you do every day, the things you do every week, and the things you do every month, quarter, and year.

Now think about what you are responsible for.

Firstly, the team of people you lead and manage.

Then any functions or processes you are responsible for.

And, what budget or resources you manage, to help you get the job done.

Next, consider what decisions you have to make as part of the job.

What can't you do? (i.e., what are the limits of your responsibility?) Think about the decisions you must get agreed or signed off by your own manager or someone else in the business.

And finally, which other teams you work with (for example because you manage different parts of a process or activity).

You might have a very long list by now, and there might be several bullet points that are similar or part of the same task or activity. It probably doesn't look much like a job description at this stage, so the next step is to group activities together and rephrase them to show what you are responsible for. If you have got several linked activities, your task is to find a way of expressing the full process from beginning to end.

For example, you might have the following linked tasks listed:

- Hold 1:1 meetings with each team member.
- Record notes of 1:1s.
- Agree targets for individuals.
- Monitor progress against targets.
- Act when someone falls below standards.

Rather than have 5 tasks, we could re-phrase this as:

- Manage performance of individual team members by agreeing and monitoring objectives, and taking corrective action as appropriate.

Now you just have one sentence, and it describes a responsibility (manage performance) by the tasks involved (setting and monitoring objectives for individuals, taking corrective action).

Continue like this until you have 6-8 key responsibilities which cover at least 90% of what you do.

If you were intending to use the job description for recruitment, you would now add a person specification. This is a list of the experience, knowledge, skills, and behaviours that an individual would have to demonstrate to be successful in the role. Some of these will be essential to the role – the job-holder cannot do the role without them, and a person would not be shortlisted for interview if they did not have them. Others will be desirable – they might help someone onto a shortlist in preference to another candidate if everything else about them was the same.

Measuring business performance with Key Performance Indicators

You may have Key Performance Indicators (usually referred to as KPIs) in your business, or you may never have heard of them. KPIs are exactly what the name suggests. The most important (key) targets, or numbers, or signs (indicators) that tell you how successfully the business is currently operating (performance).

If KPIs are chosen carefully to represent all the significant factors that make up the organisation's overall performance, they will give your organisation a good indication of whether it is on track to meet its own targets and strategic goals.

KPIs are normally a mix of lead and lag indicators. A lead indicator is something that tells you in advance how good performance is going to be, before you even achieve the performance. Sales appointments are a good example of a lead indicator – if sales appointments are higher than expected, we can predict that more sales will be achieved, and therefore we can predict that profits will be higher than anticipated.

It's also the case that KPIs can drive unwanted behaviours or outcomes. If we have spent more time or money to achieve those sales appointments, the cost per sale will have increased, and this will have the effect of lowering our profit margin. So, we also need a KPI around costs if our true aim is to maximise profits.

Costs are a lag factor. Although you can predict, or budget, for future costs, you can only measure what was actually spent after the costs are incurred. So, a lag factor tells you what you have already achieved, although it cannot predict with any degree of certainty what you will achieve in the future.

Most businesses that publish KPIs use them to focus on four key areas. Financial performance, customers, internal business processes, and learning and growth.

How is your team's performance assessed?

Measuring performance can be challenging, because not everything a team does can be measured easily. And sometimes the KPIs of the whole business don't logically translate into team targets.

Some teams have more measurables than others, and for those teams with fewer tangible outputs, justifying performance can be difficult.

As an example, it is relatively easy to measure the performance of a sales team. Most organisations will measure:

- Prospecting calls
- Leads converted
- Number of sales visits/calls

- Sales value
- Sales volume
- Sales over time.

When salaries are known, it is straightforward to calculate the cost per sale. Most companies can also predict the number of prospects needed to achieve a sale, and the lifetime value of a customer. In many sales roles it is also easy to see who is making the most calls, whose conversion rates are above or below average, who is making the high value sales, and whose income per customer is lower than average.

Now consider an administration role. You can probably count the number of emails received or invoices processed. You might know how many phone calls were taken. You can probably come to some conclusion about which administrators are more efficient and which are less so by looking at the time each administrator takes to perform certain tasks.

However, measuring other roles can be more challenging. IT and HR are prime examples. Both are cost centres, like the administrators, though the value of their contribution isn't so easily measured. For HR you might count the number of roles recruited, or the number of disciplinaries held, yet a lot of the work HR does is much less tangible. Coaching managers and succession planning are valuable activities that can increase the organisation's future potential, but it's virtually impossible to put a tangible value on this.

Similarly, the IT team may spend a large part of the year planning for and installing new equipment which improves the reliability of the organisation's systems – yet it's hard to know what that is worth to the organisation because so many of the benefits of new systems appear insignificant to users.

So, HR and IT tend to be measured and targeted with KPIs around absence, systems availability, expenditure, staff retention and training hours. Measures of failure rather than measures of success, because there are so few ways to calculate the direct value they bring to an organisation.

Whatever work your team does, you need to find something to measure your team's performance by, and then choose which of those measures to use as targets. And that will differ depending on the type of team you are managing. And the things you end up being able to measure might not feel very fair ways of assessing someone's contribution to the business. So, you need to look carefully at whether you are being fair, and what kind of behaviours your team's measures and targets are likely to drive.

What behaviours are your targets driving?

There's a management mantra, often attributed to Peter Drucker, that "What gets measured gets done".

There's no doubt in my mind that this is usually true. Nevertheless, there are two problems.

Firstly, managers normally end up measuring and targeting things that are easy to measure. These are not necessarily the things that drive performance or what is right for their organisation to achieve its goals.

And secondly, employees focus their efforts on achieving the targets that they know managers will measure. Though not necessarily in the way their manager would want them to achieve those targets.

Let's look at both via a few examples of things many organisations CAN measure and target, and some reasons why you may not be assessing what you think you are.

Clocking on/off times – it's funny just how many businesses are happy to discipline people for being a few minutes late clocking on, while ignoring side conversations, toilet trips and invented errands that use up a lot more time. Just because someone is present, it doesn't mean they are performing as they should or contributing to your business.

Log in/Log out times – surely there is no simpler way of measuring someone's performance than how long they spend logged into a computer? Except of course, being logged in does not equate to doing any work, and it is quite possible to spend many happy hours perusing the internet while logged in, and not actually doing much work at all.

Key strokes – an obvious improvement on log in/log out times – except of course that it is very easy for someone to make lots of keystrokes and do very little meaningful work.

Juuuuuuuuuuuuuuuuuuuuuuuuuuuuuuuuuuuuuuuuuuuuuuuuuuust
liiiiiiiiiiiiiiiiiiiiiiiiiiiiiiiiiiiiiiiiiiiiiiiiike
thaaaaaaaaaaaaaaaaaaaaaaaaaaaaaaaaaaaaaaaaaat.

Calls taken – the very first person I dismissed used the time after they thought managers had gone home to cut off every call they received, just after it had dropped into their headset. This meant that the call was counted as a legitimate call (even though no human had answered it) and the two or three seconds the call lasted counted towards the call handler's average call time. So, at a stroke the employee improved the number of calls taken while simultaneously reducing their average call handling time. Which put this call handler at the top of the performance charts for their call centre.

Orders processed – which can of course be processed much faster if you omit key information that others then must spend time tracking down. Or if you accept orders for things you know to be out of stock, since that's someone else's problem to resolve.

Sales – even that holy grail. Especially that holy grail. Sales are one of the easiest things to fiddle if you really want to. Converting enquiries to sales at month end, knowing they will cancel after the all-important performance figures are acquired. Selling an inappropriate solution to a customer (such as a 25-year savings plan to a 90-year-old). Or manipulating the figures by inputting individual items as separate sales rather than a single sale, or selling 24 units when you are supposed to be selling a single box of 24. Easy mistakes to make – although only, apparently, by those who are determined to mislead their employer.

Invoices processed – if you're targeting by value, you can guarantee someone will be sorting through and picking out the higher value invoices so that they are doing less work than anyone else. Or if you are measuring by volume, that same person will do their best to off-load the more complex cases to some other poor unsuspecting person.

You get the idea. If you have anything else in mind to target, you could drop me a message via my website, and I'll be happy to give you some thoughts on how your targets can be manipulated by those employees who want an easy life.

The point to remember is, you need to be careful in what you measure, how you set targets, and what behaviours you might be encouraging. And then you will need to put additional monitoring or supervision in place to ensure your targets are being achieved in the way you would want them to be. Employees are only human, and we all like a short-cut, especially if we think we won't be caught.

It's easy when a business is doing well to accept the results and not worry too much about how they are achieved. But in the long term, this strategy always fails. We become lazy, in the sense that we stop holding people to account for the way they achieve their results. Meanwhile, employees settle into a pattern of shortcutting procedures, eventually forgetting the "correct" way of doing business. They've learnt the right things to say to convince you everything is fine and stop you asking difficult questions. Bad habits, short cuts and half-truths become the norm.

Asking difficult questions isn't being unreasonable or unfair. Understanding how your part of the business operates and achieves its results is a fundamental responsibility of the management role. Looking beyond the headlines to understand the full story helps you challenge inappropriate behaviours before they escalate into something far worse.

So, what are your team doing right now? Do you really understand how last month's performance figures were achieved? What procedures were bypassed or side-stepped to hit targets? What promises were made to customers to secure their business? Do you know what, specifically, your top performers are doing differently from everyone else? Are you happy with their methods?

Your role, as a manager, is to think the unthinkable. Don't take performance figures on face value. Machine-generated performance data cannot tell you how performance is being delivered – you must watch and investigate to find out why.

And for the same reason, you need to investigate your best and worst performers. And anyone whose performance suddenly improves or deteriorates. These are major warning signs of either personal issues affecting performance, or that someone is deliberately trying to manipulate their performance data.

CHAPTER 6
KNOW YOUR TEAM

How much time should you spend getting to know your team? The answer is "a lot longer than you think".

There will always be managers who think that holding the occasional team meeting, and promptly answering email queries from their team, is enough. After all, people are there to work so what more do they expect?

The reality is, the more you know about each person in your team, the better manager you can be for them. You'll find it much easier to predict their reactions to decisions or changes in the workplace that affect them, and you will know just what to say, and how to say it, to get the best performance from each of them.

Let's look at how you can get to know your team and make an impact. I've suggested two different approaches; one for new managers, and one for people who have been managers for longer. You'll pick up some useful tips by reading both sections.

If you're a newly appointed manager

Planning for the first 3 months
A manager I worked for early in my career told me this, and I have found it to be true every time I have started a new role.

"It takes 3 months to feel as if you're being effective in a new job".

The first month will go by in a blur of faces, paperwork, meetings, and more meetings. Nothing will make much sense; you won't know what to focus on or how to achieve any significant change. And it's very likely you will feel you aren't being much help to your team. Try not to worry. No-one is expecting you to change the world immediately, but during this first month they are expecting you to rapidly assimilate a lot of information about the business and your role within it.

So, use your first 30 days in the role to learn about the culture and rules of the organisation, the basics of the systems you will be using, and to meet the people who are going to be most important to your new role. Usually the people will include:

- Your own manager,
- Your own team members (who report to you)
- Other managers who report to your manager,
- Your main internal customers and suppliers (the managers or teams inside your organisation that you will work most closely with).

Have a large notebook (at least A5 size) and make notes at every single meeting. You'll be bombarded with information and there is no way you will remember more than 2 or 3% of it unless you write it down. Have at least a page for each person you meet, each policy or report you read, each procedure you must follow, and each meeting you attend.

Focus on learning where you fit within the organisation, and what others within the business are hoping you will achieve or change. Don't worry about too much else at this stage – keep up with your emails and when you aren't in a meeting, use your time to read or talk to people about issues in the business, and be present with your team, observing what happens day to day. In the next section I'll talk about what to cover in your meetings with your team, but before I do that, I want to talk briefly about months 2 and 3.

By the end of the first month, or at least the start of the second, you will feel you are beginning to understand what needs to be done, but you'll be conscious that you aren't actually doing any of it or making much difference. I recommend that now is a good time to develop an action plan. Use your notes and observations to make a list of the key tasks or projects you need to focus on. Don't edit the list too quickly – it's better to try and capture everything first, then edit later.

Once you have your list, use the next week or two to sense-check the list with your team, your own manager, and other managers you will be working closely with. Aim to have some timescales against each of the tasks or projects, so that you know how to prioritise your time going forwards.

It doesn't matter if your action plan is for 3 months, 6 months or a year. The format isn't important either, although you should include as a minimum the task, the date it needs to be delivered, and who else might be involved in delivering it. What matters more is that you commit to achieving every agreed action on the plan. Remember to be realistic about the time you will have available – you need to fit the work on your action plan around meetings you are expected to attend, and 1:1s with your team, and at this stage in a new role it is much better to under-promise and over-deliver than to over-promise and fall short.

To make a real impact for yourself and your business, identify 3 or 4 quick wins that you are confident you can achieve before the end of month 3. They should be tasks that will make a significant difference to your team's performance or customer service.

For the rest of month 2, and all of month 3, focus your efforts on 1:1s with your team, the meetings you need to attend, achieving your quick wins, and anything else on your action plan that needs to be started or completed during month 3. Involve members of your team where you can, to help you find out more about their skills and abilities, and so they don't feel neglected as you work on your action plan.

By approaching your new job like this, you will give yourself a sense of achievement each month, and this will help your confidence to grow. Your manager will see that you are delivering what you promised, and your team will notice that you have made positive changes which have helped them perform more effectively. Most importantly, you'll begin to truly believe that you can do this job and be a success at it.

Meeting your team for the first time

It's a bit like your first day at school. You walk into a room, whether real, or virtual, and there are a bunch of faces looking at you, expectantly. Your new team. And how you behave now, on your first day, or in your first few months, will set the tone for the rest of your time as their manager.

Some managers are very tempted to make an impact on their new team, and quickly. They run in like the proverbial bull in a china shop, destroying every system, tradition or way of working known to the team, keen to impose their own methods, personality, and style on the way the team works.

The result is usually a very unhappy, unsettled, and resentful team.

Here's a secret. You are going to make an impact, whatever you do. You can decide whether you want the impression you make to be a positive, constructive one, or if you want to be seen as a bit of an idiot really.

You can make a good impression by listening. Really listening.

Make it your aim to meet with everyone in the team during your first week. But don't just book a team meeting and think that will do. Team meetings only really work for those who are confident and outgoing when surrounded by other people. Your introverted workers, and those in your team who are less socially confident, will just stare – either at you or at the table.

You need to have 1:1 meetings with each person in your team. Proper, individual conversations where you both do some talking and some listening. Book them in advance so that people have some time to think about what they want to say to you. Let them know that you want to learn about them as people, to understand their roles and to find out what challenges they have in their jobs.

And when you hold these initial 1:1 conversations, make sure you do more listening than talking. Aim to speak no more than 30% of the time, and have your new team members talking for 70% of the time. Don't jump in and tell them your plans. Use the opportunity to listen to what is going on, identify any undercurrents or tensions within the team, clearly understand what each person considers to be the problems or challenges facing them as individuals and as a team, and take lots of notes.

If you're asked what your plans are, the best way to reply is to say you want to understand how things are from the team's perspective first. Then you want to make a plan to try and tackle the problems facing the team and to help improve team performance. Show them you are on their side, and here to support them.

Some managers find it uncomfortable to talk about personal lives. Even so, I think as a minimum you should aim to find out some key things about each member of your team. I would start with their family situation (Where do they live? How do they get to work? Do they live alone or with others? Who are the significant people in their lives? Do they have children/pets/hobbies?)

This conversation should be about building some rapport between you and your team members. Finding out what you have in common, and what is different. Helping you to start to see the company and the job from the employee's perspective, and to see them as a whole person with a life and commitments outside work.

But this isn't just a social, getting to know you kind of meeting. This is also your first opportunity to find out about their role, their skills and experience. Don't make it a formal job description review, but do ask them to tell you what their role is within the team, and find out how long they have been with the company, and what they did before they joined your team. Ask them to explain to you where their work comes from and where it goes to after they have performed their part of the process. What do they like about their job, and what is their least favourite part? Who do they work well with, and is there anyone in the team they prefer not to work with? And is there anything else they think you should know?

Make notes as you go, so you don't forget who said what. Resist the urge to step into any ongoing team disputes or personal relationships. You are just watching and listening to begin with. You need to hear every side of the story before making your mind up whether it is appropriate for you to intervene. Remember, you don't want to make an impact for the wrong reasons. When you decide it is time to step into a team dispute, make sure you first read the tips in the next section about managing team conflict.

It's a good habit to have a similar discussion with every new member of your team while you are the manager, so why not make that a resolution, starting now?

When you've managed your team for a while

If you read through the previous section for new managers, and thought that there was some information in there that you still don't know about some of your team members, then perhaps now is an opportunity to think about how you do communicate with them, and whether you are as observant as you should be about what is happening within your team. Here are a few things to think about.

Team dynamics

Who is friends with whom in your team? Are they friends outside work as well as inside? How far will they go to defend and protect each other?

And if you think they are all just one big happy team, think again. Most teams have some tensions amongst members, and if you can't see it, the most likely reason is that you aren't looking hard enough. So, who avoids whom? Who isn't speaking unless they are spoken to? Do they sit together during breaks, or do some people go off on their own? Is that a problem for them, for the rest of the team, or for you? Or is it even a problem at all?

Who has the power within your team? Regardless of job role, there will be someone in the team with a stronger personality than the others, or with natural leadership qualities, who other team members look up to, and are strongly influenced by. If you can identify this individual, and work with them, your role as a manager will be much easier. Bear in mind, though, that if you make an enemy of them, you will have a permanent struggle to get the rest of the team onside with any changes you want to make.

Are they a team that agrees about most things, or are there frequent outbursts, or conflict situations? Are there cliques and how do they interact with each other?

A word about team conflict

It can be really tempting to wade into team disputes and arguments, and try to sort them out and get everyone to be happy and friendly again. You might even think that as a manager, this is your role. And to some extent it is.

However, the real secret to managing conflict is to work out when to get involved and how. Not every battle is worth winning, and a certain level of conflict within teams is actually very healthy. If people disagree about the best way to solve a problem, or introduce a new system, that is a good thing and you should encourage them to air their concerns and suggestions in a positive and constructive manner. You will invariably end up with a better solution.

Teams who agree about everything are a real worry. It's either a sign that they don't care about what is best for the business anymore, or a sign that groupthink has taken hold. Groupthink is a psychological phenomenon first identified by Irving L Janis in 1972. He observed that individual team members are often driven by a need for harmony within the team. As a result, sometimes team members may put aside their own concerns or misgivings about a decision, for the sake of team cohesion. You see groupthink where someone goes along with a team decision because they think everyone else is agreed, and they don't want to be the only negative voice. It's dangerous because people can start hiding problematic information from the rest of their team or their manager, rather than speaking out. Team members can put pressure on each other to keep quiet and not to rock the boat.

So, when everyone agrees, stop. Ask yourself whether this seems too good to be true. There is a strong possibility that it is.

Spot the signs that you need to step in and manage a conflict situation

While you should allow the team to work through conflict themselves to some extent, there may come a point where you must step in. Either because the conflict is taking up too much time and energy within the team, and they have demonstrated that they can't solve the issue themselves. Or when it becomes personal.

The role of a manager is to be a decision-maker, so if the team are taking too long to decide, you will need to make the decision for them. If they are stuck, going round in circles having the same conversations over and over and getting nowhere, then you need to intervene.

And if members of the team are picking on individuals, or bullying or victimising them for having a different opinion, you absolutely must step in and stop the situation as soon as it comes to your attention. There are formal disciplinary procedures that apply to bullying and victimisation, and you must ensure you carry out a proper investigation to determine whether disciplinary action is necessary. It's always preferable to stop the situation before it gets this far – but it's also important to recognise if it has gone too far and make sure you follow the relevant procedures to put it right.

How well do your team know each other?

I know managers who prefer to arrange work so that their team members rarely see each other, or have opportunities to work together. These managers generally lack confidence in their own ability to manage people, and are afraid that if their team members form strong personal relationships, they will become some sort of threat to the manager.

It's as short-sighted as it is ridiculous.

Businesses operate in teams because people generally perform better overall when they are working with others, and have others to bounce ideas off or solve problems with. The old saying "two heads are better than one" is true for most people in most organisations. And even when people say they prefer to work alone, most still need some human interaction with other people who are working towards the same goals.

How teams grow and develop

It is useful to bear in mind that teams go through certain stages as they get to know each other and become an effective team. This was most famously researched by Tuckman and Jensen, whose team development model is a classic management theory.

The first stage is when team members don't know each other at all. They are all very polite to each other and it is unlikely anyone is going to be 100% honest about their thoughts or feelings. No-one is sure about their own roles or anyone else's and the team probably don't have many effective procedures or systems. The manager's role is to get everyone talking to each other, and starting to build relationships. This can happen in many ways – you might consider holding more frequent team meetings, or facilitating meetings between individual members of the team, or by introducing team-building activities to help people get to know each other.

The second stage is where conflict starts to arise between team members. Because roles aren't very well understood, people may jostle for power, or try to offload work they don't want to do onto others. Things may go wrong because no-one is really sure who should be doing what, and they might start to argue with each other about who is responsible and who should resolve things. At this stage a manager's role is to talk to every member of the team to understand what is going on, and to establish how work should be structured so that responsibilities are clear and nothing falls through the cracks.

The third stage is where the manager starts to introduce some order to the team. Job roles are clarified, procedures and systems are put in place and everyone understands how work should flow through the team and who is responsible for each part of the process. Conflict reduces as the team feel more confident in what they are doing, and in the team's ability to deliver its goals.

In the fourth stage, the team are delivering all their goals, and working well together to resolve issues as they arise. The manager's role is to monitor performance and make sure everyone can continue to work to the best of their ability. The manager may become something of a trouble-shooter, resolving issues before they reach the team so that the team are able to focus on delivering results.

There can often be a fifth stage, where someone leaves the team, the team's role changes significantly, or perhaps the team is disbanded altogether. Performance may drop as the team misses the person who has left, or perhaps the team struggles to take on their new responsibilities, wishing things could go back to the way they used to be. Managers who recognise that this is a natural stage in team development can help their teams to see the benefits of this new change to the way they are working, and help them learn the skills they need to make it a success.

Tuckman and Jensen called these five stages *forming, storming, norming, performing and mourning.*

They are natural stages that every team experiences, and you cannot skip a step. You must work through each one. Some teams get stuck at one stage for months or even years, and that is always because their manager isn't moving the team along that stage quickly enough. If the team halts at the storming stage, for example, every day at work will feel like a battle. People will form cliques and some will become difficult or even obstructive if the conflict continues for too long. Bear in mind that the team can't move themselves on – they need their manager to resolve the conflict, help them determine new ways of working and push them through the change.

What many managers don't realise is that if someone does join or leave the team, or there is a significant change to the team's work (such as a major new task for the team to complete, or a substantial change in the way a task must be done) then the team will slip back through the stages. And they don't just slip back to the previous stage – they go all the way back to the first, forming stage.

If you think about it, it's obvious they must go back to the beginning. If a team member leaves, their replacement won't have exactly the same skills, experience, or attitude, however hard you try. They will have different strengths, different interests, and a different approach to the way they work. With the best will in the world, you can never find a perfect replacement. So, the team will have to get to know the new member of the team – and we're all nice to people when they first join our team, aren't we? We don't tell them what it's really like to work here – we let them find out for themselves. So, we're not 100% honest with them.

And then if they don't do things in quite the same way as their predecessor, perhaps things will slip. Maybe they will miss out a certain part of a process as they are learning, or because it isn't something they enjoy doing. So, the arguments start amongst the team, people come to the manager complaining that the new team member isn't doing their job properly and it all begins again.

Just remember this is normal. It is not a reflection of your ability to manage a team. It is purely a natural evolution of the team. Go back to the tasks you undertook last time the team was in the forming or storming stages. Hold more frequent team meetings, and help the team member to get to know each of their colleagues more quickly. Clarify job roles to take into account the new team member's strengths and weaknesses, and thrash out some new procedures or ways of working. And then you can work your way through the norming stage to become a highly performing team again – until the next change happens.

Getting the best from different team members

The best teams comprise people from different backgrounds, with diverse strengths, personalities, and experiences. These bring a range of perspectives to the organisation, which can be really helpful when considering new product offerings, improvements to customer service, problem-solving and many other aspects of business life.

It's also true that a diverse team are likely to have very different needs from you as their manager, and this may require you to use different strategies and tactics to get the best from everyone in your team, and be the kind of manager that each team member needs.

I could write about dozens of different characteristics and traits, some of which people can change, and others that are fixed. For the purposes of this section, I am just going to focus on just five types. These often cause concern for new managers, so here are some brief thoughts about how you could get the best from each team member.

The quiet one: Head down, hard at work at their desk, seldom joining in with team conversations. Often criticised for not being team players. Some people are naturally quieter than others, and as a result their contribution to the team can often be overlooked.

You will rarely get the best from a quieter employee in a team environment, so make opportunities to see them 1:1 as often as you can. If you want their help with an issue, or their contribution to a problem, you'll often get a better result if you give them advanced notice, so they can spend some quality thinking time on the issue before they speak to you about it.

The older one: New managers often worry most about older people in their teams. I think this is usually an issue of self-confidence for the new manager, and what they think an older person might feel about being managed by someone younger. The truth is you are unlikely to know how an older person feels about being managed by you, or to find out how much experience they might have, unless you ask them. It's likely that as long as you treat them as any other member of the team, they won't give your age and experience a second thought.

Stereotypes about how quickly people learn as they get older are just that – stereotypes. Everyone is different, and we can all pick up new skills at any time in our life if we are taught in ways that suit our learning styles.

Do watch and listen to how other members of the team treat older workers, and if you hear age-related "banter" act quickly to stop it. Also be sure to give all employees access to the same training and opportunities, regardless of their age.

The younger one: Younger workers often find their skills and abilities can be overlooked by managers who make assumptions about them based on their age. And an employee who joined the company from school may never be able to shake off perceptions of youthful inexperience. This can cause disillusionment at just the point in someone's career when they should be ambitious and excited.

Watching my eldest daughter and her friends prepare for their prom, I saw so many skills that are really valued in the workplace: working under pressure, juggling different priorities, team-working, keeping in touch with colleagues, planning and organising, communication, decision-making, managing change and meeting deadlines. I also witnessed qualities that any workplace would welcome – mutual support and encouragement, enthusiasm, reassurance, flexibility, and a willingness to step outside of their comfort zone.

They didn't do things the way I would have done them. Occasionally they needed advice or guidance, and they learned a lot along the way. But there's no question that they achieved, or exceeded, expectations - it was definitely "alright on the night".

You can get similar results from younger workers by giving them a clear goal, a deadline, support, resources, and a compelling reason why they should act. Ensure others in the team treat younger workers with respect, and don't allow disparaging remarks about "the youth of today". All the points above about banter and training opportunities apply equally to younger workers.

The argumentative one: Most organisations have one character who uses every opportunity to argue. It can be over something apparently trivial, such as the type of coffee in the kitchen, or a more significant change in the way the team is working, with which your argumentative team member has taken issue. Some people genuinely believe they are never at fault for anything, and their first reaction when confronted is to put up their defences and argue.

If you argue back, you are giving the individual the attention they crave. It is likely to ignite further grievances which they will be very happy to share, particularly if there is an audience listening. And that audience will be watching and listening, to see who really is in control within the team.

It is sometimes better to let the person vent. Providing no-one is likely to be hurt and nothing damaged, letting them get it all off their chest can, eventually, defuse the situation. Make sure you are standing somewhere near a door or near the middle of the room, so you have an escape route. You, as the manager, need to stay very calm and composed. Don't argue back. Try to do the opposite of whatever the employee is doing. If they are shouting, respond quietly and assertively. If they are speaking quickly, pause before you reply, and then speak slowly. Stay rational, and don't let things become personal. It's not possible to have an argument if no-one argues back.

If the behaviour continues, or becomes disruptive for the team or the business, you may need to consider whether there are ways to help the individual deal with their concerns more constructively, or you may have to resort to formal disciplinary procedures.

The troublemaker: This character may not openly challenge your position as manager, but they are likely to stir up discontent amongst the rest of the team. Perhaps they are always pointing out flaws in what you say, or problems their team are encountering because other people aren't doing their job properly. Occasionally you will encounter people who just lie, blatantly, to make things appear worse than they really are.

In my experience, troublemakers are usually bored. They can often be quite intelligent people, who aren't sufficiently challenged in their current roles. Causing chaos within the team is their way of bringing a little excitement to the working day.

Talk to them, and try to understand what is at the root of their behaviour. Is there something going on at home, or a workplace issue that you are not aware of which is affecting their judgement? Can you coach them how to deal with that situation more effectively?

Or are they bored? Could you give them more responsibility? It sounds odd to reward someone for obnoxious behaviour, but I have promoted more than one difficult person who has turned into a superstar, so it is an option worth considering.

It's a different matter if your trouble maker is leading others in the team astray, or creating an atmosphere that affects their performance. In this case you need to do two things. Firstly, remind everyone in the team of the rules, and the consequences of breaking them. And secondly give direct feedback to the ringleader that leaves them in no doubt their behaviour cannot continue. Document everything you say, and be prepared to follow through with disciplinary action if necessary.

CHAPTER 7
MANAGING YOUR TIME

I t's 9am and you've been at work for two hours already. You are still catching up on the paperwork from yesterday. There's a report that's due by lunchtime and you haven't even started on it.

You have 3 unopened emails from your boss, all of which are labelled urgent. A delivery hasn't arrived which means the team won't be able to meet their targets and deliveries to customers will be delayed. The phones aren't letting any external calls into the building. And 2 members of your team have said they need to speak to you urgently this morning, and neither of them can wait until tomorrow.

You can see how quickly and easily you can feel overwhelmed as a manager.

Why it's almost an automatic reaction to decide that it's all your team's fault, that if they didn't consume so much of your time, you would be able to submit your reports on time and keep up with your paperwork. That you are too busy doing the day job to manage a team.

And it's also easy to make the wrong choices, to focus on the wrong priorities, and to lose track of what you are actually employed to do.

And when you encounter all these challenges, at once, it's natural to go straight into reactive mode. Your mood changes, you probably become snappy (even if you aren't aware of it) and your decision-making is impaired because the levels of stress hormones in your body mean there isn't enough oxygen getting to your brain.

The secret of good management is to put some effective routines and systems in place, to minimise the likelihood of problems occurring, and to reduce the impact of those problems when they do crop up. That way, when challenges do arise, you can prioritise them with a clear head and a logical approach.

The routines I am going to suggest to you are designed to help you be a part of the team you manage, so that you know what is happening on a day to day, week to week or month to month basis. You'll be able to predict a lot of problems before they occur, which will allow you to plan how to resolve them with a calm head, rather than in panic mode.

You'll also be able to put procedures in place to prevent problems arising in the first place. If deliveries are unreliable, you could plan to increase stock holdings, or switch production to other products to ensure there is continuous work for the team. Perhaps you could plan in routine maintenance for quieter spells, to improve the reliability of the equipment your team uses. Maybe someone in the team could produce some of the data for the reports you have to write, or could handle some of the emails you receive, to free up your time.

And when your team can see there is a structure to your day, they will understand the timeslots they can rely on you being available. Then they will learn that they don't need to interrupt you every time there is a problem, only every time there is an urgent issue that cannot wait until you are next going to be available.

As a manager, your job is to manage people. You might also have a day job to do, but how much of it you do yourself, and how much you choose to delegate to your team is entirely up to you. You don't have to do all the work yourself.

Your team's job is to do the work you give them. They do have to do all the work themselves. And as we have already seen, it makes sense for them to do as much work as they can possibly do, because your organisation probably pays them less than it pays you. So, the more work you can delegate to your team, the more cost effective your team will be.

Your manager's job is to manage you. Your manager can pass all the work to you. You can choose how much of it you do, and how much you pass along to your team. If the work gets done, confidentiality is maintained appropriately, and risks are managed, your manager really doesn't care who does the work. They just want the work to get done.

If you remember those priorities, you won't go far wrong.

Let's look at some of the daily, weekly, monthly, quarterly, and annual tasks that the most successful managers do, to help them manage their teams more effectively. They might not be the tasks you are expecting to see. I'm not going to talk about to-do lists, or power meetings. I'm going to talk about the simple things you can do every day, that will build trust between you and your team. Tasks that might feel unnecessary or unimportant, although they are, in fact, the critical actions that differentiate the great managers from the indifferent and poor managers. Tasks that require very little in the way of management training, and a whole lot of being a curious, interested human being who cares about how others are doing.

Daily tasks

Say Hello

You would be seriously surprised at the number of managers who don't even bother to say "Hello" or "Good Morning" to their team members. I've known managers use the back stairs to get to their office so they didn't walk past their teams. Managers who made sure they were in work before their team members arrived, so the manager could be in their first meeting, or at least too engrossed in their work to be interrupted by the simple social niceties of morning greetings.

Check in

Hello is good. Even better is to have a few words with everyone in the team each day. Just a quick "How are things?" "What have you got on today?" or even "Did you watch the match last night?" The aims of a check in are to build relationships, give your team an opportunity to catch you if they need some help from you, and to help you spot anyone who isn't looking ok and might need some additional support from you today. If you make it a part of your daily routine – maybe wandering around while you have your first coffee, or while you are distributing work to the team – you will know the temperature within the team each day, and be aware of any bubbling issues that you might need to get involved with.

A great way to check-in quickly and consistently is to hold a daily huddle or check-in meeting. These can be an effective way of updating everyone in the team about what is going on and any changing priorities. The best huddles involve the team standing up in the middle of the team's work space. Standing up keeps the meetings short – they should take no more than 5-10 minutes, and you should aim to hold them at the same time every day. Everyone at work at that time attends. A sample agenda would include absences and how to cover them, today's priorities, and any issues the team or manager need to know about. But don't let people launch into debates or discussions. The point is for everyone to be aware of priorities and issues pertinent to the team, and for you as a manager to identify anyone who needs more of your time today. So "I'll come and speak to you shortly about that" should be your catchphrase. Huddles work equally well as short video calls, so why not try having a huddle every day for a month and see whether it could work for your team? I'm confident you'll find communication improves drastically and you'll have fewer interruptions during your working day, since people will know they will see you in the morning and can raise any non-urgent concerns then.

Allocate/redistribute work

A fundamental part of any manager's role is to make sure everyone has enough work to do, and that they are focusing on the right tasks each day in line with the organisation's priorities. It's also to spot potential bottlenecks, under-utilisation of resources, and other challenges which team members may not be able to resolve themselves. You may also need to redistribute work if someone has called in sick.

You may have the type of team where you need to give out work every day, or you may have a team that deals with tasks as they arrive from customers. Either way you should be keeping check on who is doing what, any backlogs forming, who has spare capacity and who is struggling with issues and needs your support to resolve them. Remember your team members might not tell you when they have an issue they think they can resolve themselves, or they may not even recognise they have a problem. Since you will know what is going on in the rest of the team, you may be able to identify problems before your team can.

You can do this just as easily for a remote team as for a team that are located in the same building as you. Face-to-face you can simply walk around and observe what is happening. Remotely, pick up the phone and talk to people. Especially if you are in the habit of distributing work via email. The phone gives you a much better opportunity for a two-way conversation, which in turn will help you to establish how things are really going, rather than how you think they are going.

Walk the floor

If the start of your working day was the time for saying hello, checking in and distributing work, the second half of the day needs to be about making sure things are going to plan.

If your team are in the same place as you, this part of the job is quite easy. You just need to get up and go for a walk. Stop by and see how each person is getting on. Nothing heavy, you are just letting them know you are there, you are available to help if needed, and you are still interested in what they are doing.

With a remote team it will take a bit more thought. You could pick up the phone again ("Just thought I'd check in and see how you are doing with …") or you could set up an afternoon drop-in session via your video calling software. Again, don't make it a big deal – just have a call open at an agreed time, and let your team know that if they need to update you or need some help, they can pop on the call and you will be there to talk to. Keep a note of who joins the call and who doesn't. On a day-to-day basis it doesn't really matter if someone doesn't participate, but over the course of two or three weeks if someone consistently doesn't show up for the call, give them a ring and check in on them. There might be a very logical explanation (picking children up from school, taking calls, or they don't currently need any help) or there might be a problem brewing that you need to know about, and a call is the best way of making sure all is well.

Review completed work

Your final task each day is to review the tasks completed during the day, and use this information to update your workplan, and decide how you will allocate work tomorrow.

Who has done well today? Who is stuck? Who has been side-tracked onto other tasks? What are you going to do tomorrow to make sure everyone understands their priorities and can focus on completing the work the team needs towards its KPIs?

Weekly tasks

The good news about weekly tasks is that – if you have completed your daily tasks every day – these should be very quick and straightforward to complete.

Your weekly tasks are an opportunity to step back and review the bigger picture. A time to see how the team's daily activities have made a difference across the week. You'll be using the daily checks you have been doing for most of these weekly tasks.

Review team performance against plan

How have your team performed overall this week? Did they hit all their targets? Did their performance improve from the previous week? What challenges did they face, and how well did they cope with them? What have you learned about your team this week, and what have the team learned that will improve their future performance?

Make a few notes and keep them on your computer or in your diary. These will be useful for team appraisals, and for reporting back to your own manager about your team's progress.

Check individual performance

On the same lines as the team performance, look at the individuals within the team and how they have performed across the week. Can you see any patterns emerging around individual performance? Are some people consistently better on certain days of the week? Or at certain times of the month? Are there differences in performance between people working remotely compared to those in the workplace? Are there some tasks that are slowing the team down more than they should? How can you address this – more training, or more support for the team?

Celebrate team and individual wins

It's important to take time out to notice and celebrate success for individuals and for the team. If they are working hard and delivering their goals then you owe it to them to say thank you in some way. Now is not the time to let the team think you are an ungrateful slave driver!

Your team will perform better, and more consistently, if they understand that you notice and appreciate their hard work. So why not make an event of it? There are plenty of ways of recognising performance that don't have to cost a lot.

Perhaps you could have an employee of the week award? Or you could buy cakes or biscuits for the team to recognise when they have all had a good week? Many companies now offer hampers and other gift ideas for remote workers, so there is no reason why they should miss out on any goodies. Other ideas include team breakfasts on a Friday morning, or letting people go home early at the end of the week.

The important thing is to recognise people consistently, and to reward appropriately. Biscuits and cakes are worth a lot less than time off at the end of the day, so save the more valuable rewards for the genuinely special achievements.

And don't overlook the impact of a very simple, heartfelt "Thank you". Or a written email or letter of thanks from you, or even better, a more senior manager.

Most people like to be noticed, and they love to feel appreciated. So, make sure that you recognise people every week, for the small things as well as the big achievements. And remember that some people hate to be the centre of attention, although they will still appreciate a personal note or gift. Just so long as it isn't presented in front of the rest of the team.

Plan for next week

It's easy to get so tied up in the day-to-day activity of the team that you forget to think ahead, and plan for the future. As a manager you should always be looking forwards. What are the performance outputs required from your team next week? How many people are available to deliver them? Which of your hybrid workers will be in the office, and when? Who is sick, or on holiday? What are the various deadlines you'll have to meet, and what bottlenecks or other issues might they cause? Who do you need to spend more time with next week? What will your own week look like, and when can you carve out time for your team members to see you?

Monthly tasks

1:1 appointments with each team member

I could write a book about all the benefits having regular 1:1s with your team will bring you. It might feel like time you cannot afford, but you really will start to understand the value of them in a very short space of time.

Once your employees realise they will see you every month, for up to an hour at a time, you will find they need to interrupt you less during the normal working day. They will learn to save non-urgent problems until their 1:1 when you can have a productive conversation about how to resolve them. You will also learn more about your employees – what they enjoy or dislike about their jobs, what is going on outside of work for them, and what's happening between them and the rest of the team. You'll find out things that you could never have discovered while chatting in the office, and they will help you improve the performance of the team, and become a better manager.

I suggest seeing each member of your team once a month, as a starting point. Whether the meeting is face-to-face, or online doesn't really matter. In either case you should be in a private office or meeting room, with no other distractions. That means phones off, and no sneaky reading of your emails while you are supposed to be listening to your employee speak.

As a minimum, cover these topics.

- Action points from the last meeting – have they all been achieved?
- Current work in progress – check to see these are still priorities, and whether the individual needs any support from you to achieve them.
- Work for the next month – some of this may come from the employee, though most of it will probably come from you.
- Development/support needed by the employee to achieve the work required in the next month.
- Any other business.

Make sure you keep a record of what was discussed at each 1:1. A time-saving tip is to get your team to write up their own 1:1 notes, and send them to you for approval/signature. They only write up one set of notes each month, and they have a personal stake in getting them right, and you just need to check they have included everything you discussed. (Bear in mind, when tempted to skip the check and just sign the form, that it's not unknown for employees to "forget" to include tasks they don't want to perform).

Your final task regarding 1:1s is to make sure you and your team have dates for the next month in your diary, and that these dates still fit with the needs of the business.

Update personal files for each employee

Notes from 1:1 meetings should be stored in personal files. Whether these are paper-based or computer-based doesn't matter, but you must make sure you store all sensitive personal data in accordance with the GDPR requirements. That means they should be locked away securely, and you should only keep accurate, factual information. Remember that employees can request to see any information written about them, so make sure if yours ever do, they'll only see information they already know exists, and that is objective and accurate.

Check team overtime, holidays, and sickness

As you are going through personal files or records, this is a good time to get your diary out and check overtime against budget (if relevant to you) and how your team are doing with using their holiday entitlement. You don't want to get to the end of the year and find everyone has holiday to use up, so making sure everyone has some holiday booked, and checking if they have used roughly the right proportion of their leave for the time of year is an important task that you should complete regularly.

Now is also the time to review your team's absence records, and identify whether any individuals have reached a level of absence that triggers an informal meeting or a formal absence review. Anyone who has been off sick for more than a week should have a regular welfare call from you – these need to go into your diary for the next month.

Quarterly tasks

Review individual performance against objectives

If you have been having regular, monthly 1:1s, this task will be straightforward. You can carry out a review during your normal 1:1 – it should just take a couple of minutes in most cases, maybe longer if the individual is having problems with any of their objectives. Of course, if you have been doing the 1:1s each month, you will already know what challenges your team members are facing, and you will already have action plans in place to help them to succeed. So, this quarterly review is simply a case of summarising and agreeing with your team member how they have progressed so far, and what actions they need to take next.

Depending on the size of your team, you might also want to map out how each team member is performing against each of their objectives. You might be able to identify some trends, or some problems for the business if several objectives have been delayed. A mapping exercise is always a useful activity for you as a team manager, because it will effectively show you how you, as the manager, are performing in your role. So, it will give you all the evidence you need for your own performance review with your manager.

I hope this helps you see that what might, at first glance, appear to be a time-consuming task gives you:

- An up-to-date picture of your team's performance.
- An action plan for each team member of development or support needed to achieve their goals.
- An action plan for you of the areas where you need to intervene to help your team achieve its goals.
- The evidence for your own performance review.

So that's one task, with four concrete and useful results. A great example of how good management practice enables you to leverage your time as a manager.

Annual tasks

Appraisals

I'm using the term "Appraisal" because annual appraisals are still a common feature in small businesses. If you work in a larger organisation, you might have more regular, less formal performance conversations.

Personally, I don't think the name or the frequency is terribly important. What really matters is that some sort of formal discussion takes place regularly to assess employees' performance over an agreed period of time, agree targets and give feedback, and that a record is kept of this discussion. These discussions may feed into pay reviews so it is important that they are taken seriously.

If you have carried out 1:1s and quarterly reviews throughout the year as I have suggested, the appraisal process becomes a whole lot easier, quicker, and more effective for you and your team members.

Whether your company appraisal process requires it or not, I always recommend getting your team members to complete a self-assessment before the appraisal meeting.

A self-assessment is an opportunity for the employee to gather all the evidence they have about their performance during the year, to review it, and to summarise how they think they have performed. Many employees don't understand the point of a self-assessment, or how to go about it, so you will need to give them some guidance on what you expect.

Your company may have a specific form for self-assessment, or if they don't, you could give each team member a blank copy of the appraisal form, and ask them to complete it.

The sort of evidence employees could look for includes:

- A list of all the different activities they have been involved in across the year. Not just work topics, also include project groups, focus groups, or personal development they have undertaken
- Emails or records from projects they have undertaken during the year. It is important to encourage employees to think about everything they have achieved during the year – not just their objectives, but the other side projects and additional responsibilities they have taken on since their last appraisal.
- Feedback from other managers or teams, or from customers, about the employee's performance.
- Examples of where they have used their initiative, changed a process, or implemented a new idea, and how these have improved their own or the team's performance.

- Any other training or development they have undertaken during the year, and how they have used this to improve their own performance.
- Their ideas for future objectives, training, and support for the next appraisal year.

Not everything on this list will be relevant for your team, so pick the things that will help you both come to a fair assessment of their performance. You could also suggest that they attempt to rate themselves before the appraisal meeting. This will be useful for you, as it will highlight any major differences of opinion, and enable you to spend the appraisal meeting focusing on the most important areas.

Ask your employee to send you their self-assessment 24 hours before the appraisal meeting. You should find that they include much of the information and evidence you were planning to discuss, which means these areas can be quickly agreed.

You may also find they put forward information or evidence you had forgotten about. In which case you have an opportunity to reassess your own rating for the individual.

And that just leaves any areas that the individual has forgotten about, or where you disagree on ratings, for discussion during the appraisal meeting.

Development and succession planning
This should follow your appraisals with each member of your team, and is an exercise that is ideally carried out with other managers in the business.

The purpose of succession planning is to help you identify the individuals who can move into new roles over the next 6-36 months. In a perfect world, you would have a successor in mind for every supervisory or management level role in the business, and for every professional role within the business too. And each of those identified successors would have a development plan to help them get from the role they currently have to the role that has been identified as their next step.

Development planning is for everyone in your business. I am a firm believer that every employee must be encouraged to continually develop their skills so that they keep up with the changing demands of their role, their customers, and the wider business. You can create an expectation within your team that everyone must improve their skills every year, and you can lead by example by developing yourself, and encouraging everyone to have some training, or learn a new skill each year. Development plans are the written record of what training or development each individual is going to receive, when it is going to be delivered, by whom, and what support the employee will need before and after their training has been completed, so that they can embed their learning and the employer can benefit from their new skills.

Make these daily, weekly, monthly, and annual tasks your routine, and you will always know how your team are performing, what help they need from you, and what capacity they have for taking on new tasks. You'll always know whether you can commit to that rush job, or a change of working practices, because you'll know what time and skills you have available within the team.

And best of all, you'll feel like you know what you are doing. Your days will have a structure, problems will be flagged earlier, and your team will want to help you to resolve them because they have learned that you can be trusted to look after them and look out for them.

CHAPTER 8
MANAGING REMOTE TEAMS

There is a widespread belief amongst some managers that leading a remote team is more difficult than managing a team who all work from the same location. And many businesses were quick to declare that "Remote working doesn't work for us", even after their employees worked successfully from home for several months during the Covid-19 pandemic.

Managing a remote team is different, certainly. It requires another way of thinking, and planning time for managers and teams. There are distinct challenges that co-located teams don't share, as well as advantages you don't see when everyone is in the same workplace. There are new skills for managers to learn. None of these are difficult unless you choose to make them so.

Of course, there will always be jobs that have to be performed face-to-face in a workplace. You can't be a retail assistant, a carer, or operate a production line working from home. And there are many other roles that require a presence in a particular location or the job simply cannot be done.

But there are many tasks that can be done from home, at least some of the time. And in this chapter, we are going to explore what you need to do differently when managing people in different locations, so that you can make remote working a success in your organisation.

There's a lot of jargon associated with remote teams, so here is a quick summary of terminology I will be using, and what it means.

Co-located teams	Teams who sit together in the same workplace location.
Dispersed team	A team that is geographically spread out, perhaps working in other corporate buildings or locations, or in client offices, or working from home.
Flexible working	Any working arrangement that involves different hours or location from full-time working. Can include part-time, hybrid working, annualised hours, compressed hours, and many other non-standard work patterns.
Hybrid working	A flexible working arrangement where the employee works some of the week at home, and the rest of the week in their normal workplace.
Inputs	The time and effort someone gives to their work.
Outputs	The results or deliverables of an employee's work, such as reports written or tasks completed.
Remote working	Any working arrangement where the employee is not required to perform their job at the employer's premises. Can include working from home, from hotels or other coworking spaces.

The advantages of remote working

Reduced costs – Employees save on commuting costs, while for some employers remote working can offer the opportunity to downsize office space.

Employee motivation – Many employees report that remote working increases their motivation. Some of this comes with the autonomy they gain when working in isolation, including the ability to control how they structure their working day. Motivation can also be a result of feeling trusted by their manager to work remotely, and from the time they gain by not commuting to and from work.

Increased productivity – In roles that require a lot of thinking, the opportunity to work without interruptions can result in much improved productivity. Some workers will also enjoy the challenge of powering through their work to finish a bit earlier.

Healthier workplaces – reducing the number of social contacts people have will reduce the transmission of bugs and viruses that otherwise make people ill. No manager wants to have Covid-19 circulating in their workplace, with all the associated disruption to trading and potential long-term effects on employee health. Many employers have reported much reduced absence levels amongst employees working from home. Whether this is a good thing (people are becoming ill less often) or a bad thing (people are struggling on when they should really be taking time off sick) remains to be seen.

Reduced employee turnover – Flexible working is one of the most sought-after benefits according to job applicants. It stands to reason those employers offering remote working will retain employees who value this way of working

The challenges of remote working

Are they really working? – Some managers simply don't trust their workers. Others want to trust them, but don't know how. Being able to assess how much work someone is doing when you can't physically see them is a skill that many managers lack.

Communication – How do you keep lines of communication open when you don't see people at their desks or bump into them at the water-cooler? There's no question that it takes more effort to communicate with remote workers, but with the right routine and methods you can communicate effectively and make sure no-one feels left out of important decisions.

Some workers can be at a particular disadvantage – Young workers, workers with disabilities, and female workers have all been reported to be disproportionately disadvantaged by working from home when compared to a workplace.

For young workers, the issues are that there is often a lack of suitable space for homeworking, and that being away from more experienced team members and managers may limit their opportunities to develop new skills, network and make new connections, and attend external events such as conferences or training.

The concerns for women and people with disabilities are that lack of visibility in the workplace might reduce opportunities for promotion and career progression. Being out of sight may also result in them being out of mind as far as their managers are concerned.

Unhealthy working patterns – There are real risks that workers may be working much longer hours than they would in the office. The lack of normal cues, such as other people leaving the office at the end of the normal working day may be a factor for some who simply lose track of how long they are working. Others may fear being thought of as underperforming, or could have far too much work. It may be easier to hide this from managers when working from home.

Team-working and team spirit – With limited opportunities to get together, and many video-conferencing packages only allowing one person to speak at a time, it can be challenging to create the sort of camaraderie and mutual dependence that co-located workers often enjoy. Misunderstandings can lead to conflict and it is important that managers think carefully how to create team-building opportunities for remote workers.

As you can see from the advantages and challenges above, there is plenty to consider when managing a remote team. Much will depend on whether you, as a manager, can put the right personal routines and structures in place to make remote working function effectively for everyone. Once again, you are in control, and you can make it a success by remembering and implementing some key actions.

8 ways to make a success of remote working

1.   Understand what makes co-located working successful
Although this may seem an odd place to start, it is useful to think carefully about the dynamics of co-location, and which of these might be absent for your own remote team. Then you can focus your efforts on actions that will compensate for the missing elements.

Some of the advantages often cited by managers and team members include:

- Being able to see what others are working on.
- Stopping at someone's desk to ask a question.
- Bouncing ideas off others.
- Side conversations before, during or after meetings.
- Spotting that someone is unhappy/overworked/not busy/feeling left out.

- Overhearing a conversation and joining in.
- Watching team dynamics – who speaks to whom? How do people interact? Who is ignoring whom?

You can probably think of others so add them to your own list.

What you might notice about my list is that all these happen quite naturally in the workplace. With remote working, managers must plan opportunities for spontaneity. Which sounds like a contradiction, but by making sure people can have informal, unstructured conversations during their working time, you can replicate some of those chance encounters that we value so much.

If your list includes items relating to technology working better in the office than remotely, perhaps this is something to investigate further? Could your organisation benefit from upgrading its technology to help remote workers be more productive? Some managers will dismiss this out of hand, assuming it will be far too expensive, without fully investigating the costs and benefits. There are often new, more cost-effective solutions available that could even be cheaper than the technology you currently use. You'll never know unless you research the options.

2. Remember your values and culture

Whatever approach you decide to take must fit with your organisational culture and values, as well as your own personal values. So, think about these carefully, and consider how they will translate into a dispersed team. For example, if you have an organisational value relating to team-working or collaboration, it is going to be particularly important that you create lots of opportunities for people to work together, even though they are in different locations.

Perhaps you have a value relating to innovation? How could you encourage innovation without the usual office chit-chat and bouncing ideas around? If inclusion is a value, how will you make sure remote workers feel included in important decisions that affect them or their work?

3. Understand each team member's outside commitments

I've talked about this earlier, in chapter 6, and I think with remote teams it is even more important to understand what is going on in your team members' lives outside of work. Who has children, elderly relatives or pets that need attention during the working day? Who lives with other people and may have difficulty concentrating during meetings while others are in the house? Who has medical conditions that make them tired at certain times of the day? Who struggles with technology or has an unreliable internet connection? This is not an exhaustive list, but it does give you some ideas of who you might need to think about when organising work and communicating with team members.

4. Be proactive

As with any other team, the success or failure of a remote team mostly rests with the manager. If you sit back and expect things to run smoothly and produce the same results as a co-located team, you and your team will be very disappointed.

So, get on the front foot. Think about the different ways your team needs to communicate, and work out how you can replicate these for a remote team. For instance, you will need to consider:

- *Formal events* such as team meetings, 1:1s, appraisals, cross-department meetings, and company communications.
- *Informal opportunities* like coffee-break catch-ups, meetings for general queries, co-working sessions, social events during or after work,
- How to manage *ad hoc meetings* so that people aren't overwhelmed by meetings to the extent they cannot complete their own work.

You may also want to consider whether to set some boundaries around start and finish times, length of meetings and number of attendees.

I would recommend having a team communication plan, which sets out what meetings will happen, when, who needs to attend, and how teams should communicate with each other outside of these meetings. Involving your team in putting this plan together will help to get their buy-in and avoid any conflicts or attendance issues. You might want to include some agreed "non-meeting" times so that people can plan their work and other responsibilities knowing that they won't be disturbed.

5. Control meetings carefully

Running successful meetings online, or with a hybrid team where some attendees are in the workplace and others join online, requires a different level of organisation and structure compared with face-to-face meetings.

Attention spans are shorter for online attendees. It's more difficult to pick up body language cues if you are only able to see the heads and shoulders of other people in the meeting, and it is easier to "zone out" during parts of the meeting that aren't relevant. Add in the normal distractions of working from home, such as pets, the doorbell ringing or children arriving home from school, and it quickly becomes obvious that meetings will need to be run differently.

As a general rule, online meetings should be shorter than face-to-face meetings, and only those who have to be there should attend. If you do find you need a longer meeting, tell attendees at the beginning of the meeting what time they can expect a comfort break.

Plan the agenda carefully, and circulate it at least 24 hours before the meeting. This will give everyone time to think about what they want to contribute.

Agree expected team member behaviours during meetings. For example, you could agree that all meetings must start and end at the published time. Should cameras be on or off? What preparation must people do before the meeting? What should attendees do if an urgent email arrives during the meeting? Who is responsible for taking notes and what are the timescales for publishing the minutes or action points?

Aim to start each meeting with a short "human to human" check-in. Think about the sorts of things people discuss while waiting for face-to-face meetings to start. Last night's TV or football match, something in the news, or even what sort of biscuits everyone is eating. If you are really stuck, do an internet search for ice-breaker questions, and have some fun at the start of your meetings. It will help people to feel connected and to believe you care.

During the meeting, make sure everyone gets an opportunity to speak without interruption. Ask questions to encourage participation, and invite attendees to use the "raise hand" feature to indicate they wish to speak. Use your power as host to mute people if necessary, so that everyone can hear clearly. Notice who doesn't say as much as others, or anyone who looks distracted or unhappy and be sure to catch up with them after the meeting to check they are OK and discuss any concerns.

End meetings on time so that people who need to be somewhere else can be at their next appointment on time. And remember to send each attendee the minutes/action points at the end of each meeting.

6. Be flexible

If someone was in a face-to-face meeting with you and their laptop stopped working, what would your first thought be? Usually we feel sympathy for the individual, and will offer help to get them back up and running. We can see immediately that the problem is the technology rather than the user.

It might surprise you then to observe your reactions the next time a remote worker cannot log into a meeting because their broadband is down, or their laptop is updating. Or they can't get screen-sharing to work. I've watched many meeting hosts automatically assume the individual has done something wrong. It's probably the geographical distance that changes our assumptions and creates barriers between us, but it is something to keep in mind with your team.

Recognise that sometimes broadband goes down, systems don't work as quickly or effectively at home, or children won't entertain themselves, and support your employees to catch up when they can.

7. Think differently about performance

Many managers have an innate dislike of remote working because they find it difficult to assess how people are performing.

It's so easy when people are in the workplace with you. You can see how much time they spend at their desk. The paperwork moving from one side of the workstation to the other. You can hear their fingers tapping on the keyboard, and you can feel confident that they are working hard, and all is well.

Managers like to have their teams where they can see and hear them. It means they get so much more work from their employees.

Except, of course, none of these comforting signs offer any guarantee that a person is doing any productive work.

And anyway, whose performance is better for the organisation? The person who spends 8 hours at their desk reading and sending emails, or the one who spends 3 hours working from home to resolve a problem that will save your business thousands of pounds? Should you reward the person who starts work on the dot of 8:30am and rings 20 prospects who all say no, or the person who starts work later but makes 3 big sales before lunchtime?

Thinking differently about performance means judging people by the outputs they produce, rather than the inputs. Or put another way, by their results rather than the amount of time they spent achieving them.

Some examples of outputs you could use to reassure yourself about performance include
- Number of calls made
- Number of sales closed
- Revenue received
- Quality of reports submitted
- Projects delivered on time and on budget.

(You might like to refer to Chapter 5 for a reminder about measuring team performance).

Assessing outputs rather than inputs also means you can be more flexible about the hours people work during the day or evening, as long as targets are achieved. You don't need to pull people up for not being logged into their computer at 8:32am because it doesn't matter what time they work, only that they get the results.

The exception to this is, of course, where you need to cover incoming phone calls and email inboxes during standard working hours. Where this is the case, work with your team to agree how they will cover rather than expecting everyone to be available all day.

8. Be inclusive

Make sure your remote working employees aren't out of sight and out of mind. You need to ensure they have opportunities to learn new skills, mix with people outside their immediate team and achieve their career goals. This might mean making time for them to access online training during normal working hours (just as an office-based employee would access face-to-face training during the working day). Or facilitating their attendance at cross-departmental meetings or on projects involving other teams.

In many respects hybrid working, where employees work some days in the office and the rest of their week at home, can offer the best of both worlds in terms of an inclusive environment. For employees, hybrid working can offer opportunities to stay connected with work colleagues and attend important meetings while also managing their responsibilities outside work.

For people who live far away from the workplace, or who struggle to physically get to work because of a health condition or disability, a job in which you only commute a couple of days a week is likely to be much more manageable, and therefore attractive, than a role requiring attendance 5 days per week.

Some companies have decided to hold all their large meetings online on a permanent basis. Their business case is around the time and cost savings of people not having to travel to meetings, and many have also found online meetings more inclusive. With everyone sitting in the same sized box on a screen, and only one person able to speak at a time, it can help quieter employees to feel more confident about contributing.

In conclusion, managing hybrid teams and remote workers doesn't have to be difficult but it does require a different mindset for you as a manager, and a different focus during your working day. I hope with this knowledge it should be much easier for you to allow more flexible or hybrid working within your team in the future.

CHAPTER 9
WORKING WITH OTHER MANAGERS

If you are working in a larger organisation where there are several other people at management level, you will need to consider how you are going to work with those other managers to drive your business forward.

Management team dynamics can make for very interesting times. And I use the word "interesting" quite deliberately.

On the face of it you are all managers working for the same business. You all have the same ultimate goals which will be to ensure the business achieves its profit targets, and to put it in the best position to survive long into the future.

You all have a relationship with each other, and must rely on each other to deliver each part of the business operations; that way, the company can operate as efficiently and effectively as possible, while making the maximum returns on investment for the business owner.

Sadly, in some organisations, it can feel as if the management team are pulling in opposite directions. Information isn't shared quickly or openly. Those who shout loudest get the most investment, while those whose voices aren't heard find their departments falling behind.

Stronger personalities can dominate decision-making while quieter, constructive criticism can be ignored. Longer-serving managers may feel their time in role gives them a seniority over other management team members way beyond that implied by their job position.

Left unchecked, power struggles can lead to dysfunctional behaviours and ultimately can cause considerable damage to the culture, performance, and long-term prospects of the business.

Even management teams need a strong manager, to ensure the business comes first rather than managers' egos.

What can you do if your management team is dysfunctional?

This is ultimately the responsibility of the business owner or managing director, but there are some steps you can take as an individual manager to help the management team you are a member of become more effective.

Don't pretend to know everything – contrary to popular belief, it is obvious when someone is bluffing or "winging it". Ironically, it will make you look more foolish than simply admitting you don't know something and asking for help. Learn from those who have more experience than you, and recognise that their strengths are a great advantage to you and the wider organisation. You have strengths too. Your manager saw something in you that made them think you were worthy of the job you now have. And your management colleagues may be feeling just as nervous of your strengths as you may be feeling about theirs.

Start as you mean to go on. It is important, for your mental health, to be your real self in the workplace. Well, maybe a slightly more polished version of your real self. The sort of manager who is genuine, operates with integrity, and reacts predictably to issues and challenges. Managers who play games, manipulate others, or work to their own agenda get found out in the end. It's just not worth it.

Play your part – by understanding your own role you will know how you should be contributing to the success of the business.

Build channels of communication – you may not need to speak to some managers every day, but you should make sure you meet with them all on a regular basis, and not just in formal management meetings. Schedule time to have catch up meetings with each manager on a 1:1 basis, ideally monthly or at the very least quarterly, where you can focus on getting to understand what they do, their challenges, their plans for their part of the business, and how your respective teams can work more effectively together. And remember to share your own plans and challenges too, so that you can work together to build the best business possible.

Stand up for your team – they need someone to have their backs, and that person is you. You will need to be your team's advocate and defender, shouting about their achievements and making sure they are given a fair share of the work and the rewards of the business.

Keep up to date with what is happening in other parts of the business, so you can share information with your team and be sure they hear what is happening in the company from you, rather than on the grapevine. If you don't understand whether a change affects your team, ask for more information. If you know a change will affect your team, make sure you are involved in discussions around developing and implementing the plans for the change, so that your team's concerns and needs can be addressed before the change hits them.

Try to resolve issues with other managers yourself, before going to your manager. The school playground saying that "nobody likes a snitch" still applies in the workplace. And every confidential conversation becomes public knowledge at some point. Become a problem solver, look for ways to work with other managers to collaborate and achieve outcomes that suit everyone.

If you do feel the need to talk to your manager about tensions within the management team, try to talk about the work-related issues, and keep personalities out of the discussion as far as you can. Explain how your team's work processes are affected by what is going on. Or how customer service might deteriorate, or discuss your concerns about quality or costs. Do try not to make it personal. Remember, every member of your management team is sticking up for their team, doing their best to deliver their objectives, and trying to help the company survive long term. Just like you.

Remember that you're not going to like – or be liked by – everyone. Even so, don't let personality clashes destroy a professional relationship. Keep things civil, polite, and measured. Look for ways to build others up, rather than knock them down.

And if things don't improve, remember that life is too short to be miserable in a job. No job is worth your family life, your health, or your sanity.

Managing your own manager

Now the idea of managing your own manager might sound a bit strange, so bear with me on this one.

Because the relationship you have with your own manager is going to be the most important indicator of how successful – and how happy – you are going to be in a management role.

If you are very lucky, you have a manager who has learned what works and what doesn't, who is self-aware and understands their own strengths and weaknesses, and is emotionally intelligent enough to be able to recognise the impact their instructions or actions might have on the people who report to them.

Unfortunately, the chances are that they aren't a perfect manager themselves. They may never have been trained in how to manage people, and so lack confidence in how to do the job well. And their lack of confidence may make them wary of others who they see as a potential threat to their position – the person who could step into their shoes, so to speak.

So, don't assume they know how to do the job of managing people any better than you do. And don't assume that what you see must be what you get. There are ways of managing the relationship you have with your manager, how you behave and how they respond, that will make your working life a lot easier and more enjoyable.

Let me start with some examples – all from real life, from people who have been on management courses with me in the past. I have changed the names...though everything else is as they described.

They interrupt me at the same time, every day

Barbara loved her job. She was very self-motivated and personally very organised. But she really struggled with her manager who wasn't as organised – or perhaps wasn't personally organised in the same way as Barbara.

Barbara said to me "I come into work at 8:45am, check the messages, make a coffee, sit down and start my first task by 9am. And every morning without fail, at 9.15am, my manager comes and sits on my desk, interrupting what I am doing, and giving me a whole lot more work which completely messes up my plan for the day."

I couldn't help myself.

"Barbara, if you know that your manager is going to come to you at 9.15am every day, have you thought about scheduling yourself to do a few two-minute jobs at 9am, while you are waiting for your manager to come and tell you what their priorities for the day are at 9.15am?

And then plan the rest of your day when you know what your manager needs you to do?"

I'm convinced that idea had never crossed Barbara's mind at all.

And in truth, I think many of us are like Barbara. We have our own preferences for the way we like to work, and we put our own routines in place to suit ourselves. We then become fixed into a way of working that we prefer, and which works for us, and can't see any reason why we should change.

So, when we start working closely with someone who has different routines and preferences, we get very frustrated with "them". We think "they" are the ones who should change, to fit in with our way of working. When actually, we could take control of the situation by adapting the way we work to fit in with others.

Changing your working style and behaviour to suit your own manager isn't really any different to changing your management style and your approach for each person who reports to you.

My manager can't make a decision
Robert was a very outgoing sales manager. And like many good sales people, he loved to talk. He was always on the go, and he didn't like paperwork one little bit.

His manager, Allan, was the complete opposite. He was very quiet and thoughtful. He was always reading, or writing detailed emails to colleagues and clients.

"Allan just can't make a decision. I go into his office every month for my review, and I usually have several issues that I need him to sign off on. Discounts for clients, changes to credit lines, quotes that are outside what we normally offer, or changes to the way I want to run my team. I never get a decision from him. It's driving me mad".

Robert's was a typical example of a clash of thinking styles. Being extroverted, Robert didn't like detail. He wanted to be able to bounce an idea around for a couple of minutes and get a decision. Because that was the way he made decisions himself.

Allan had a more introverted style of thinking. He liked to have all the facts in front of him, and plenty of time to digest those facts, find some more data, and then reach a decision confident that he had thoroughly researched every angle. He felt uncomfortable when Robert tried to bounce him into a decision without any warning, and with evidence amounting to no more than a gut feeling and a couple of conversations. Allan generally responded by shutting down completely, and refusing to consider the issue at all.

Robert would have a better relationship with Allan, and would be more likely to get his ideas and proposals approved, if he adapted the way he presented information to Allan. I suggested to Robert that he sent Allan an email three or four days before the next meeting, outlining any decisions he wanted Allan to make during their review meeting. If Robert also sent some background research to support his ideas, Allan would have time to think the idea through. He could check Robert's research and do his own fact-finding, putting him in a much better position to make a decision on the day.

I've seen this scenario play out in reverse, also. The keen manager who writes a detailed report for their own boss on a topic that needs a decision, only to find when they get to the meeting, that the boss hasn't read the report and just wants to hear a summary of the key points. Imagine how that feels, having perhaps spent a couple of days putting a report together, to find it ignored. Would you be surprised if they became disillusioned and demotivated, feeling that their hard work isn't appreciated or respected?

You can get upset or frustrated wishing others would change, or you can change your own approach and get better results from others. Which will most help your job satisfaction and career development?

They micromanage me – I can't do anything without permission
My absolute, heartfelt sympathies go out to you if this is your manager.

In my career, this is the very worst kind of manager I have ever had the misfortune to work for.

The manager who must sign off every decision or action, because they don't trust anyone to do things as well as they do.

Who keeps their team members in their place, refusing to allow them freedom of thought, or freedom to shine, in case the team member outshines the manager.

Who doesn't teach their team members new skills, or allow them any personal development, because they don't want the team member to be promotable.

Micromanagers come in all shapes and sizes. Some are clock-watchers, some know every HR policy and rule that can trip their employees and don't hesitate to use them (while happily ignoring the rules themselves) and the worst, I think, are the nit-pickers. I had one manager who would never allow a document to leave the team unless she had amended it. She even "corrected" spellings and made them wrong, and all documents had to go out in her name so that she got the credit for them.

If they weren't so soul-destroying to work for, I would have a lot of sympathy for micro-managers. They are people with shockingly poor levels of self-awareness or self-confidence. They're always overpromoted and always terrified they will be found out.

In many cases, you can learn to live with them. If you understand they are always scared of getting things wrong, you can make sure the research and preparatory work you do is thorough, and they have plenty of opportunities to review it in a timely way.

If they ask you several times a day for updates on how you are progressing with a particular task, it's a sign they are nervous that a deadline is going to be missed. So, take it as a hint that you need to check the priority for any new task they ask you to do, and where it fits with the other work you have already been allocated. And send them regular updates of your work in progress, so that they know you are on track and don't need to keep asking.

If they want to sign everything off before it leaves the department, it means they are nervous of making mistakes. So, ask them in advance to specify exactly what needs to be done so they can sign it off first time.

If they clock-watch, understand that this is a form of control they can exert when they feel out of control themselves. I'm not sure there is any way of dealing with this, other than being very punctual yourself, and not giving them any cause for complaint that you aren't working your contracted hours.

If you struggle to get time in their diary, it's probably because they over-commit their time to try and show the rest of the world what a huge workload they can manage. Watch their routine, and work out when they are most likely to be sat at their desk, and have an impromptu meeting with them.

If these tactics don't work, then your only options are to live with it, or to find another job. Micromanagers who cannot be "cured" or "managed" out of their addiction to controlling every aspect of their team's work will eventually destroy the self-confidence of every member of their team. They will have everyone second-guessing every move, paralysed into inaction by the certain knowledge that anything they do outside of the strict parameters their micro-manager has set for them will be rejected or overturned.

Incurable micromanagers are toxic. They eventually poison everything around them, destroying the morale of the whole team. Avoid, avoid, avoid!

My manager gives me no direction or feedback at all

Kathy's manager, Tom, was at the other end of the scale entirely.

Kathy had never had a 1:1 with Tom, in nearly 2 years since she started the role. Whenever she asked, Tom said he employed professionals, and he expected them to get on with the job they were employed to do. He didn't have time to mollycoddle so if Kathy couldn't do the job, then she knew where the door was.

The truth was that Tom didn't feel at all confident about managing people. His coping mechanism was to avoid interactions with his team as much as he possibly could. He didn't see that he could add anything to the team, and nor did he see it was his role to do so. His day job was much more interesting to him than the trivial queries his team brought to him, so he filled his time with meetings and activities that would keep him as far from the team as possible.

In management terms, we would describe this style as "laissez-faire" which is French for "allow to do" or leaving things to take their own course.

Laissez-faire managers aren't all like Kathy's boss. Many haven't made a conscious decision to leave people to get on with the job as best they can. Often, they are overworked and overwhelmed, and simply cannot find time to spend with team members. Or they might have switched off from the job and be biding their time until they can leave. Some are just plain lazy.

Some employees are quite happy to be given the freedom to do their own thing, but most team members need some structure, someone to make decisions and to give them feedback on how to improve.

If your manager isn't giving you any of these things, then it's worth thinking about whether you could create them for yourself. Setting your own timetable, so that you know the important tasks will be done on time. Understanding the way decisions are made in your organisation so you can have more confidence that you are considering the right things when reaching your decisions. Or perhaps asking for feedback from your team, or from other managers you work with closely.

Kathy's biggest challenge was that she felt she had no-one to support her and fight her corner when she needed additional resources or an important decision to be made. She worked hard to make her team a success, but needed help to develop some additional skills to improve her own effectiveness. She believed the organisation was missing out on opportunities because Tom wouldn't make himself available to talk to her. And the stronger personalities in the team were starting to dominate everyone else – including Kathy.

I recommended to Kathy that she tried to speak to Tom's boss and explain her concerns, or, failing that, another manager within the business who she trusted. In bigger organisations, the HR team can help to resolve a situation like this by coaching the manager to improve their people skills, or by taking steps to remove the people management aspects of their role.

Laissez-faire management styles can be appropriate in situations where the team are very experienced, targets and expectations are clear, and the team has the knowledge and skills to be able to support itself.

But new managers usually prefer a more hands-on style of management, at least initially. Don't be afraid to ask for help, and if that support is not forthcoming from your own manager, seek it out from others within the business.

5 Steps to managing your manager

I'm going to assume that you are looking for an easy life, in which your manager behaves predictably and largely leaves you alone to do the job you are paid to do to the best of your ability.

I'm also going to assume you understand that for anyone to trust you as an employee, they must have confidence that, when they aren't watching, you are doing your job the way it should be done, that you are delivering a quality product or service to the required deadlines and making decisions in line with company policy.

Which is exactly what it takes for you to be able to trust your team members.

So, these steps will help you to identify what your manager needs from you to feel confident, and how you can take more control of the relationship by adapting your behaviour to meet your manager's needs.

Step 1

Observe carefully the way your manager works, paying particular attention to the things they do that really frustrate you or make your working life difficult. Make a list. It might take you several days or even weeks, but every time you feel your hackles rising, write down what happened, what your manager did or said and what you did or said in return.

Step 2

Using your list, identify exactly what the differences are between your style and your manager's style, and work out the most common flashpoints. What is going on when you get frustrated or when your manager gets frustrated with you? Try and think of the feelings you are experiencing, and the thoughts that are going through your head.

Step 3

Now think about your manager. What do you think is going on for them? You are not allowed to say "they are trying to make my life a misery" or "they are being difficult for the sake of it" or anything similarly negative. I want you to really think about what is going on in their head, and what emotion is driving their behaviour. As a clue, the emotion is normally fear, so what do you think they are afraid of, and why? (P.S. "Because they are an idiot" is also not a valid answer!)

Step 4

Having named the emotion driving your manager's behaviour, now create a list of ways that you could adapt your behaviour so that the emotion isn't triggered for your manager. If the emotion is fear, then your manager might need reassurance, or more involvement in what you are doing, or more communication from you to keep them in the loop so they don't need to worry that you're going to miss a deadline or forget an important part of the job.

You might need some help to come up with alternative ways of adapting your behaviour, so ask someone you trust who isn't involved – your partner or a friend outside work perhaps.

Step 5

Keep talking to your manager. Make a point of talking to them before you start a project or a new task, to understand exactly what their requirements are. Write things down so you don't forget. And agree to send them a daily, or weekly update (and agree the time/day you will send these) so that they don't have to keep asking you for feedback.

In most cases, you will find these 5 steps do ease the situation and reduce the tension around working relationships. It will take time and patience to see a difference in the way your manager behaves. Stick with it for at least 3 months. And then review whether your working relationship has improved. If it hasn't, you have three choices. The first is to accept this is how things will be. The second is to try steps 1-5 again. And the third is to find a different manager you will be able to work with more effectively.

CHAPTER 10
RECRUITING THE RIGHT PEOPLE

N ot all managers will be responsible for recruiting people, so if this isn't part of your role, you might want to skip along to the next chapter.

But if you're a business owner, or a manager in a small business, recruitment is likely to be a key aspect of your job. Getting it right will get you the talented, committed employees you are looking for who will help your business move up a level. Making a mistake can cost you dearly, not just financially but in time, energy, and your confidence levels. And imagine the impact the wrong person could have on your team.

Why do some employees change personality between interview and recruitment?

We've all seen it happen. The applicant who ticks all the right boxes during the recruitment process, is offered the job, and then turns into the original toxic employee within 6-12 months.

Or who cannot perform the job to the level required, regardless of how much training you offer them, or how much support they get from the rest of the team.

And as a manager, you might consider you are justified in feeling let down, betrayed or unable to trust any applicant again.

But how long did you really spend throughout the recruitment process testing different aspects of the employee's experience and attitude? Did you make your decision based on a 30-minute interview? Or an hour? Did you really give yourself long enough to find out enough about the employee's history or personality?

Be honest. I bet there was doubt in your mind when you made the decision to offer the job to this employee – even if it was only a nagging feeling, or something you chose to ignore. I reckon you knew you were taking a chance, and just hoped for the best.

Most recruitment decisions are not much more than a throw of the dice. Especially those only based on interviews. If your gambles tend to work out more often than they don't, that's good luck, not good judgement.

So, let's look at this again, in terms of what control you as a manager have over this situation, and how you – yes you – can make sure the outcome of every recruitment decision is the right one.

How to get recruitment right (most of the time)

1) **All managers involved in the recruitment process need training in interviewing and selection skills**

Interviewing isn't a skill we are all born with. It takes real planning and careful consideration of the key requirements of the job to interview effectively. And an ability to probe beyond the first answer given, to really dig deep and understand exactly what the employee is telling you and, equally importantly, what they are not telling you. It's also important that the managers involved understand the legislation around equality and diversity, and can structure questions in a way that does not discriminate unlawfully against candidates with protected characteristics.

Training also gives managers confidence that they are following a fair and lawful process, the knowledge of how to ask the right questions without breaching any equality legislation, and the understanding of how to differentiate fairly between different candidates. A confident interviewer can help shy candidates open up, close vocal candidates down, and identify when they have enough information to make a decision. And they will be able to record interviews and outcomes in a way that protects your business if any disgruntled applicant decides to complain.

2) You need to invest a lot of time

Most managers don't put anything like enough effort into recruiting new employees.

They think that half a day sifting through applications, and a day of interviewing is more than enough of their valuable time to invest in the process.

But ask yourself this. If you were investing in a piece of machinery or office equipment that was going to cost you at least £20,000 per year to run, with an open-ended contract that could only be terminated with notice, and which would have a fixed plus variable amount of down-time each year, how much time and energy would you invest in researching whether you were spending your money wisely? How many ways would you want to assess that kit before you spent your money? How many other business owners would you want to talk to about their experiences of the item you were planning to buy?

Would you make a purchase decision because "It's available to buy today and I think it will do?"

And yet, so many managers have told me they recruited someone because they were "desperate" or "the applicant had a pulse" or "I needed bums on seats".

It's almost guaranteed that a poorly performing employee was recruited in a hurry, with a cursory recruitment process involving little more than a quick scan of a CV and a single interview – or even two interviews – because they couldn't afford the time to do any more.

Recruitment is a critical process. It's more important than just about anything else a people manager does. Getting the right people in your business will make life easier, your team happier, and your business more profitable. Get it wrong, and you will lose good staff, a lot of time and a huge amount of money.

And you need to spend time on every part of the process. Getting the job description, person specification and job advert right, and finding the right places to advertise so that you'll attract the right calibre of applicant. Shortlisting and arranging interviews. Planning the questions you will ask, and how you will record the answers. Ordering the teas and coffees. Meeting and greeting. And after the interviews, pulling all the notes together, deciding who to appoint and notifying all the interviewees of the outcome, references, making an offer, following up references, organising equipment and desk space for your new starter, onboarding…

Recruitment done well is a big job. On average it can take 4-5 months from the point of deciding you need to recruit, to inducting your new employee. Saving time by shortcutting any of the steps will cost you a lot more in the long run.

3) You need a range of selection activities.

As suggested in the previous point, interviews are notoriously unreliable when they are the only selection activity in a recruitment process. To make your chances of a successful hire greater, you need to consider a wider variety of selection exercises, to give you a more rounded picture of each candidate.

Adding in a work-related activity will make things slightly better, and a psychometric test – which is an online or paper test that helps you objectively identify skills, knowledge, and personality traits of candidates - will improve your chances again. The reality is, it's not really the tool you use to select applicants that matters – each of them used alone are only marginally better than tossing a coin. Using several different tools together, though, will make a big difference. And the more assessment techniques you use, the greater your chances of identifying all the skills and competencies required for the job, and so making a successful appointment. So, without a doubt, for more senior appointments you should be using more selection activities than for more junior roles.

4) You must make sure your selection activities are fair.

The real test of any selection activity is whether it discriminates between people who won't be successful and people who will. That is the point of any recruitment activity, after all – to discriminate (in the dictionary sense of recognising a difference, or differentiating between people).

Of course, some forms of discrimination are unlawful. In the UK the Equality Act 2010 specifies 9 protected characteristics, which are age, disability, gender reassignment, marriage and civil partnership, pregnancy and maternity, race, religion or belief, sex, and sexual orientation.

If you choose assessment activities, or ask questions, which put people with a protected characteristic at a disadvantage compared to others without that protected characteristic, you will be breaking the law. And a tribunal claim is a very real possibility.

The safest approach is to design assessment activities around the job the person is being employed to do. So, if manual handling is a significant part of the job, you can assess their manual handling ability. But you must also bear in mind any reasonable adjustments that could be made to manual handling requirements within the job to enable someone who might struggle with physical activity to perform. That might include thinking about whether the job-holder must personally carry out manual handling, or if someone else could do it. Could you use mechanical aids to reduce the need for manual handling? Is it something that forms a large part of their role, or just an occasional activity?

Alternatively, if the manual handling in a job only actually involves getting a big box of paperwork down from a high shelf once a month, then it wouldn't be fair or reasonable to test for that during the selection process. It's not a significant part of the job. Someone else could get the box down. The box could be stored in a different place. The material in the box could be scanned and stored on the computer so that no-one needs to lift the box (and if it's that heavy, your risk assessment should have identified this and you should have measures in place to reduce the risks).

Similarly, assessing someone's reading and writing skills is acceptable if the tasks being tested form a significant part of the job they are applying to do. So, if the only things the job holder is expected to read are labels on a shelf, test whether the applicants can read the different labels. If the job involves typing up reports or correspondence, or accurate data entry, then of course you can test report writing skills or data entry.

Applicants aren't going to complain about tests that provide a legitimate assessment of their ability to do the tasks the job involves. However, if they are scratching their heads to see the direct relevance of a test for the role they have applied for, you either haven't described the job accurately, or you are testing a skill that just isn't relevant.

If you're not sure whether an assessment activity is fair – it probably isn't. So, think about how you could adapt it to make it less likely to unlawfully discriminate against a particular protected characteristic. If there are questions you are intending to ask only of females, think again.

In short, can you confidently explain how the assessment activity, or question you propose to use relates directly to the responsibilities and competencies of the role? If not, you need to adopt a different approach.

5) You need to ask the right questions

Whether you prefer formal interviews where managers sit behind desks and fire pre-prepared questions at candidates, or a casual chat, the types of questions you ask and the way you ask them can make a big difference.

These days there are two main schools of thought about interview questions. For the past 30 years or so most interviewers have preferred competency-based interviewing, which tries to pinpoint what people can do. The idea is to identify the key competencies a successful job-holder would need to have, and ask questions to test the extent to which each applicant can demonstrate each of the competencies. Typical questions start with "Tell me about a time when you…" and might end with "dealt with a difficult customer/had to reschedule your day at short notice/worked as part of a team" for example. You might probe answers further by asking who else was involved, why their solution worked, or what they learned from the experience.

The theory behind competency-based interviewing is that the way someone has tackled an issue in the past is a good predictor of how they will tackle similar issues in the future. The drawbacks are that this type of interview has become so commonplace that it is relatively easy for people to predict questions and plan their answers. Interviewers need to probe answers to establish whether the circumstances (such as levels of support or resources) were different, and to decide whether the example given is real or invented.

In recent years, strengths-based interviews have become much more popular. These aim to identify what candidates enjoy doing. You might ask questions such as "What do you enjoy about your job? Or "What tasks are usually left unfinished on your to-do list?" or "Describe a successful day?"

From the interviewer's perspective, you are looking to see how closely your vacancy matches the strengths and preferences of the applicant. Because the questions are more personal, they are harder to prepare for, especially as a skilled interviewer will move from question to question relatively quickly, meaning the candidate must think on their feet.

Whatever type of questions you choose, there are 4 things to remember:
- Ask each candidate the same starting questions (but probe differently, according to their answers).
- Test each answer so you understand exactly what the candidate's role was in each example they give.
- Look out for candidates saying "we" rather than "I". Some will do this because they saw themselves as part of a team achieving a goal together, others because they didn't actually do the thing they are

describing. Someone else did it. Challenge each use of "We" by asking "And what was your role?"

- You are looking for a rounded view of the candidate's experience. If their answers contradict each other, or there is more than one question they struggle to answer adequately, these are red flags. Another concern is if their answers use the same examples repeatedly, which could suggest very limited experience. Think very carefully about whether they have the right experience for the job.

6) Think carefully about outsourcing recruitment

Recruitment agencies will tell you they can take all the hassle and aggravation out of the recruitment process for you. They will tell you they can find the right candidate – they'll no doubt tell you the perfect candidate is on their books already. And they will tell you it can all be done so quickly you'll have that post filled in a couple of weeks.

And maybe they will.

Although it's just as likely they won't.

Recruitment has changed a lot over the past 20 or so years. It has gone from an integral part of an internal HR department, to a function in its own right. That has also brought a divergence in approach from the way HR teams used to manage recruitment, and that divergence hasn't always had positive results.

On the positive side, an agency will have professional recruiters, who spend all day searching for and assessing candidates. They may be able to offer a range of initial assessment activities that are way beyond what the average small business could afford to invest in. And they will know where to find candidates. There is no disputing that recruitment agencies can take a lot of the legwork out of recruitment.

But. And it is a big but. Recruitment agencies tend not to employ many HR specialists. Although they may call each other HR professionals, the role essentially is a sales job. Signing up employers looking to recruit, finding applicants and convincing them to put their names forward, encouraging employers to interview the applicants they have found, influencing the employer to offer the role to one of their candidates, and talking candidates into accepting the position. Because most recruitment agencies are paid for filling a vacancy.

They don't have the same drive as the employer to make sure it is the right applicant. If the applicant stays in their role for the time specified in the recruitment agency's terms and conditions, the agency will get their fee.

That doesn't make recruitment agencies a bad option, but you do need to be realistic about what they are in business for, and the service you are likely to get from them. Agencies can be a great option if you need to recruit high volumes of people in short timescales. Or if you are looking for a professional with a specific set of skills that may not be easy to find.

If you are a small business owner, with a limited budget, and not a lot of experience in recruiting, going to an agency may not be your best option. In that scenario I would always recommend using an HR Consultant to help you put together the job description, person specification and recruitment strategy to find the right applicant for your business. They might do that strategic work and then recommend you use a recruiter, or they might also offer to recruit with you and coach you through the process, so that next time you can feel more confident running the process yourself. And a big advantage of working with an HR Consultant like myself is that we can help you to understand what is different or unique about the recruitment market for your industry, and can also pinpoint any development areas in your own recruitment practice, ensuring you continuously improve your own skills and make better decisions for your business.

7) Involve your team

Team dynamics are critical to the success of your business, so making sure a new recruit will be a good "fit" is very important. Think about ways you could involve your team in the recruitment process. It could be something as simple as greeting applicants in reception and walking them to the interview, asking a few generic questions like "how was your journey?" or "have you come far?" to help settle the candidate and get a first impression of their personality.

For more involvement, you could get some team members to attend part of the selection process, for example if the candidate is giving a presentation, the team could be the audience.
Never use the team's impressions as a deciding factor in the recruitment decision – but seeing how someone interacts with others could help you to strengthen the decision to recruit or reject a candidate.

8) Do the paperwork promptly

If you are running multiple interviews for a position, and asking everyone the same basic or starter questions, you'll want a way of recording their answers so you can compare candidates. The easiest way to do this is to design a question sheet with space for you to note down their responses to each question. Use one copy of the question sheet for each candidate. At the end of all the interviews, it's helpful to have a summary sheet where you can score each candidate, and record why you are or are not offering them the job.

And I expect you are thinking this sounds like a real pain, will take far too long and surely it can't all be necessary? Besides which, you'll never need to look at it again once the successful candidate is appointed.

There are many reasons why keeping the paperwork will save you time and money in the longer run. Memories fade, and play tricks on you.

Imagine interviewing 6 candidates in a day. That's tough going for most interviewers. You're fresh and alert for the first candidate, but by the time you have seen two or three uninspiring applicants, your shoulders will be dropping and you'll be wishing the day would end.

Unless you complete your notes after each candidate, with a summary of strengths and weaknesses as you observed them, you will find that you struggle to remember what each candidate said. While you may remember the best candidate, and the last one you saw, it's very likely that the 3 or 4 candidates in the middle have merged into one and you can't remember any specifics about them. Or you muddle them so that you credit the wrong person with certain answers.

And if you recruit over several days, it's a lot harder to compare candidates because your memory of exactly how well someone answered a question last week is unlikely to be accurate enough to fairly compare them with the candidate you saw this morning.

So, completing the paperwork during and immediately after each interview will help you in lots of ways, including:

- If rejected candidates challenge why they weren't selected, the paperwork gives you evidence of the specific strengths and weaknesses of each candidate, so that you can confidently give feedback and leave the candidate with the impression that their application was managed professionally and fairly.

- If the appointed candidate turns down the role, or leaves during probation, you can go back and review other candidates to see if you could make an offer without interviewing again.

- Unsuccessful probation could be an indication that something was wrong with your selection criteria, the assessment process, or your interviewing skills, so the paperwork may help you learn from the experience.

- If you need to recruit to a similar role again, you don't need to reinvent the whole recruitment process. You will be able to pinpoint the interview questions or selection techniques that were particularly helpful or which need to be changed.

- If the worst should happen and a candidate lodges a tribunal claim alleging unfair discrimination, your completed paperwork will help you defend your actions, showing that you conducted the assessment process fairly and professionally.

9) Keep all your candidates informed

Candidates spend a lot of time applying for jobs. And often their applications fall into an abyss. It's bad enough to apply and hear nothing. But when a candidate has been for an interview, it's unforgivable not to give them the courtesy of a quick email or phone call to let them know they have not been successful. Especially if the candidate has incurred expenses attending the interview.

It looks bad on the employer, and the candidate is likely to tell their family and friends how they were treated. Even worse, they might share their experiences on social media. Which might reach your existing or potential customers, let alone potential applicants for employment.

A rejection email doesn't have to be War and Peace. A simple *"Thank you for taking the time to attend an interview with us. Unfortunately, on this occasion your application was not successful"* will be enough to allow the candidate to move on. And because so few companies do this nowadays, you'll stand out as the kind of company a candidate would want to recommend to their family and friends.

CHAPTER 11
MANAGING PEOPLE AND THE LAW

I'll be honest, I debated whether to include this chapter. Not because the law isn't important – of course it is. More because I firmly believe that if you manage people in the way I have described throughout this book, you will naturally be leading your team in a way that complies with – and mostly surpasses - everything the law requires of you as an employer.

And let's face it, very few people go into management wanting to become legal experts. So, in this chapter I am going to look at some of the biggest concerns managers have about employment law. And I'll explain what you don't need to worry about – and what you do – as well as running through some of the key things that could trip you up if you don't do them correctly.

Are Employment Tribunals really a big threat to your business?

A lot of HR people, and employment lawyers, will try to scare you with statistics about tribunal claims, and companies who have been bankrupted by tribunal awards. And if you read headlines in the newspapers about people being awarded 6-figure sums as compensation for being unfairly dismissed, you might think this is a very real threat. You might be terrified of having a simple conversation with someone who is underperforming, for fear that you may end up in a tribunal yourself, and faced with a six-figure pay-out for saying the wrong thing at the wrong time.

The truth is, huge awards are rare. They usually involve a long history of dreadful behaviour by the employer, and an employee who was on a very good salary.

The Ministry of Justice publishes data every year on the tribunal awards granted during the previous financial year. At the time of writing the most recent data we have refers to the year 1st April 2019 – 31st March 2020. This covered dismissals that happened pre-Covid-19 so is the last "normal" period for claims.

And in that whole year, there were 103,984 employment tribunal claims made against employers.

That's in an economy with 22.6 million paid employees, working in 1.41 million organisations, with over 11.8 million of those employees working for employers with fewer than 10 employees.

So realistically, your chances of being taken to an employment tribunal are very, very low.

And you can reduce your chances even further by managing in the way that a decent, caring, and considerate human being would operate; communicating regularly with your team, treating them as individuals, and doing the other things I have described earlier in this book.

It's an approach that doesn't suit large HR consultancies wanting to sell you their expensive HR retainers and Employment Tribunal insurance.

However, it makes absolute sense for your business. In nearly 30 years of working in HR, I have never been to an employment tribunal, and

I don't intend to start now.

That doesn't mean I don't take difficult decisions. I've dismissed several hundred people throughout my career. It's often not what you do that lands you in an Employment Tribunal – it's the way you do it.

You need to act fairly.

Tell people the rules, and make sure the rules are written down in HR policies that are designed to fit your business needs.

Re-brief the rules regularly, at least once a year, because people do forget. Keep a record of when and who you have briefed.

If problems occur, investigate all the circumstances. Check the written rules for any ambiguity. Also look for your evidence that the employee had been told the rules, and understood them.

Then follow your policies to the letter. If your organisation doesn't have a written disciplinary procedure, follow the steps in the ACAS Code of Practice on Disciplinary and Grievance Procedures which can be downloaded free of charge from the ACAS website.

It might sound like a lot of effort; it is nothing compared to the time and energy that a tribunal hearing would involve.

An employee who wants to make a claim in an employment tribunal must first apply to ACAS for early mediation. This gives the employer a chance to put things right if there were any mistakes made during the process, or you think you might have acted too hastily. Often, when you have sent all your evidence to ACAS, and they have spoken to your former employee, the strength of your case can put off a lot of opportunistic litigants, so it is well worth taking part in the process.

Don't allow the fear of a possible tribunal to stop you from taking action if an employee is underperforming, is toxic, or has done something which destroys your trust in them. Just make sure you follow your own disciplinary process to the letter.

Remember, managers who act fairly and reasonably, and in line with their own procedures, are very unlikely to ever face a tribunal.

Why does it take so long to dismiss someone?

As an HR professional, I think one of the hardest conversations I have with managers is the one that goes:

"I understand that this individual has been underperforming for the last 3 years. And I understand that you are at the end of your tether, and want the employee out of the business now. But you have no written proof that you have ever told them what you expect of them, or that their performance isn't acceptable. No emails. No standard-setting discussions. No appraisals. No warnings. And until you have some of those in place, any dismissal would be very easy to challenge in a tribunal, and you would lose."

As we've seen in the previous example, the law requires that employers act reasonably. That you follow certain steps to make sure that the employee understands their employment is at risk, is given a chance to state their case, and that you, as a manager, act fairly in considering the evidence the employee puts forward before making your decision.

So how do you avoid getting into this situation yourself?

Carry out the weekly, monthly, quarterly, and annual routines I set out in Chapter 7.

Keep a written account of any feedback you give to employees about their performance, and review your notes regularly. And as soon as you see a pattern, or you identify a problem, have a conversation with your team member. Tell them what they are doing, and what extra they need to do to be performing at an acceptable level. Send them an email summarising your conversation, or make a file note of your conversation and make sure they sign a copy of it.

Most employees will improve immediately. They just needed a bit of direction and encouragement. Others may need a Personal Improvement Plan to show them you are serious about the changes they need to make.

For those who still don't improve, you have the evidence in place that you have had the conversation, and they are aware of their shortcomings. So, you can then move ahead to the formal performance or capability process, confident that you have done the necessary groundwork.

It takes a lot less than 3 years if you do it the right way!

Surely I can just sack **someone on the spot if they've done something really bad?**

You can never sack someone "on the spot" under UK law.

You can dismiss someone with no notice if they commit a single act of gross misconduct, as long as you follow a fair process.

What would a fair process entail? Well, the key ingredients are:

- Being able to show that the employee had been told about the types of behaviour that the organisation considers to be gross misconduct. These are normally things like theft, fighting, fraud, major health and safety errors, bullying and harassment and so on. Most employers will have examples of misconduct and gross misconduct listed in their disciplinary policy. And we have previously talked about the importance of repeating briefings regularly to aid recollection.

- Carrying out a full investigation, including speaking to witnesses and the employee. Be prepared to speak to other witnesses if the employee brings them to your attention. If you think the employee's presence at work may hamper a fair investigation, they should be suspended on full pay for the duration of the investigation. This needs to be confirmed in writing to the employee.

- If you decide a disciplinary hearing is necessary, the invitation should be in writing. The letter should include the allegations being considered, the individual's right to be accompanied, and if their employment is at risk this should also be made clear. You should also send the employee copies of all the evidence you intend to rely on in the disciplinary hearing, anonymised only if you need to protect the identity of another employee or third party.

- Hold the disciplinary hearing, ensuring there is a note-taker present, and that the employee is given the opportunity to state their case. Where the organisation is large enough to employ more than one manager, it is good practice to have different managers carrying out the investigation and the disciplinary hearing.

- Allow the employee the right to appeal against the outcome of the disciplinary hearing. Where possible this should be to a manager who has not been involved in the case so far. In small organisations where there aren't enough managers to have a different one at each stage, it is acceptable for one manager to investigate, hear the disciplinary and the appeal. To show that you are trying to give the employee a fair hearing at each stage it can be helpful to involve an independent third party, such as an HR Consultant, during the disciplinary hearing, and perhaps a different HR Consultant to hear the appeal.

Is it true that you can't contact an employee who is on sick leave?

You absolutely can, and you most definitely should stay in contact with your employees while they are absent from work due to sickness.

The only exception is where you have been advised by medical professionals not to make contact. Even here, you should enquire whether it is possible to write to the employee, or to speak with a family member on their behalf.

If you are paying sick pay to an employee, you have a duty to check they are genuinely sick. More than this, as a good employer you have a duty of care to support your employees through periods of sickness absence, and help them to return to work.

It's quite common for employees to become anxious about returning to work. They will be wondering whether they can cope with their normal hours and duties. What other colleagues might say when they return to work. What has changed since they went off sick and whether they will be able to get up to speed within an acceptable time. An ongoing conversation with their manager gives them the opportunity to raise those concerns and have them addressed quickly, rather than lingering and causing their anxiety to grow.

You won't need to ring them every day. But try to speak once a week, and don't leave it more than a fortnight between calls. Arrange times with the employee that suit their circumstances (perhaps they need to sleep in the afternoons, or feel unwell for an hour after taking medication, or would like to have a family member present when they speak to you).

The care and concern you show for your employees while they are off sick will often be the difference between welcoming back a loyal and committed team member, or creating a disenchanted employee.

CHAPTER 12
THE LAST WORD

As you can see, being a manager isn't easy. It needs a whole new way of looking at other people, at yourself and at your business.

When you manage in the way I suggest, magical things happen.

Your team learn, quickly, that they can trust you. And when they trust you, they will tell you things that will help you to manage them even better. You will learn who is having a difficult time at home, which customers are being awkward, what's going wrong with your newest product, and which processes don't quite work the way they were designed to work.

You'll find out more quickly about issues that could derail your business, such as complaints, late deliveries, missed deadlines and other challenges, which means you will be able to tackle them at an earlier stage, when they are much easier to resolve.

You'll discover more about each team member's ambitions and fears, which will help you to be the manager they need you to be. Maybe you'll be coaching one team member to learn a new process, another to become a confident public speaker, and a third to improve their performance in their current role. Most of all you will be learning that your team members do, generally, do their very best for you every day they are at work. That when performance dips, there is always a reason and it's usually one that you can resolve, as their manager. And you'll understand how much they rely on you to remove the barriers that stop them from performing even better.

You'll be a better manager by letting your team teach you what they need, and how to respond to them. And you'll create the kind of team where people flourish and grow, because they know they are being led by someone who cares about them as unique human beings, as well as for what they bring to the business. Someone who will have their backs if things go wrong, because you communicate so well with the team that you not only understand exactly what caused things to go wrong, you led your team through the crisis and helped them put in place the measures to ensure everyone learned from it.

There is nothing about managing a team of people that cannot be resolved through communicating more often, more deeply, and more openly with the members of your team. It's that real human connection that is the difference between team members who love their work and want to stay, and those who become toxic because they feel unappreciated and misunderstood.

So don't worry about the minutiae of your HR processes and procedures. They aren't what makes a great manager (although they definitely do help).

You don't need a university degree, or any kind of management qualification.

It doesn't even matter if you get it wrong now and again. Most of us learn more from our mistakes than our successes.

You just need to talk to people. If all you do, as a result of reading this book, is have more conversations with your team, then you will become a better manager, and this was a book worth reading – and writing. If you can also consciously treat your team as they would wish to be treated - as adults who want to do a good job – then you will be the manager your teams remember for all the right reasons.

To be a great manager, you need to give your team the most precious gifts of all – your time, the space they need to be able to do a good job, and your confidence that they will deliver exactly that.

If you don't have time to manage a team because you are too busy doing the day job, then understand this.

Managing a team **IS** your day job.

And the more time you spend with your team, the better your team will become.

FURTHER READING

Here is a list of some of my favourite, go-to resources for management advice or ideas. These are in no particular order, and I make no apologies whatsoever for putting my own blog at the top of the list!

Websites

www.marionparrish.com/blog where I write about a variety of management topics.

https://www.acas.org.uk/ offering a range of resources to help you manage people legally.

https://www.bbc.com/worklife/tags/worklife *"BBC Worklife travels the world to find stories that help develop fresh perspectives on what work and life can and should be, and discover new and interesting approaches to shaping ourselves and those around us."*

Books

HBR's 10 Must Reads 2020: The Definitive Management Ideas of the Year from Harvard Business Review (with bonus article "How CEOs Manage Time" by Michael E. Porter and Nitin Nohria)

How to Win Friends and Influence People by Dale Carnegie – one of the first books I read about how to communicate effectively with people. It may be old, but it has stood the test of time.

Start with Why: How Great Leaders Inspire Everyone to Take Action by Simon Sinek

The Chimp Paradox by Steve Peters

The One Minute Manager by Kenneth Blanchard Ph.D. and Spencer Johnson M.D.

The 7 Habits of Highly Effective People: Powerful Lessons in Personal Change by Stephen R. Covey

ABOUT THE AUTHOR

Some people find their "for life" career after many false starts. That wasn't how it worked out for Marion Parrish. She graduated from The University of Bradford in 1991 with an honours degree in Managerial Sciences, and has coached, trained, developed, and supported managers ever since.

She became a Graduate Member of the Chartered Institute of Personnel and Development (CIPD) in 1996 after completing a post-graduate diploma in Personnel Management, and became a Chartered Member shortly afterwards. Her dissertation was even called "Can Line Managers Manage?"

And of course, during her corporate life working in HR roles for BT Plc, AIG, Boots The Chemists and the Learning and Skills Council, she had managers too. Some were brilliant. Others less so. Both inspired this book in their different ways.

She went on to deliver and assess Institute of Leadership and Management qualifications for hundreds of managers from director level to aspiring managers, across dozens of industries.

Marion started her own HR Consultancy in 2015, working with small businesses in the East Midlands. She saw a gap for highly targeted, 1:1 coaching for people managers, and The Accidental Manager Coach was born.

Alongside her HR consultancy work, Marion offers a bespoke 1:1 coaching programme for business owners and team managers, which aims to develop confident managers, create great working environments, and transform morale, productivity, and performance across their organisations.

.

Printed in Great Britain
by Amazon